Flow: The Feelings Of A Poet

Lavell Harris

Published in the United States of America

ISBN: 978-1-7358010-7-0 (SC)

Lavris Publishing

222 West 6th Street

Suite 400, San Pedro, CA, 90731

www.stellarliterary.com

Ordering Information and Rights Permission:

Quantity sales. Special discounts might be available on quantity purchases by corporations, associations, and others. For details, contact the publisher at the address above.

For Book Rights Adaptation and other Rights Permission. Call us at toll free 1-888-945-8513 or send us email at admin@stellarliteray.com.

Contents

LOVE VS. LUST 7

I'll Wait For You 8

I'm Not Afraid 11

I'm So Into You 13

Just Once 15

Lost In Time 18

Nerd 21

Paradise 23

She Loves Me, She Loves Me Not 26

The Walk 29

What's Love? 30

THINKING OUT LOUD 35

12 Years Straight 36

Four Walls 38

A Dream 41

Am I My Brother's Keeper? 44

Appreciated 46

Brighter Days 50

Don't 52

Electronic 55

I AM 57

I Just Want To Express Myself 64

I Just Want To Make You Proud 67

I Rise 70

I'm Sorry 73

I'm Not Perfect 76

Journey 79

Laughing 82

Let's Take A Trip 83

MY Story 86

My Turtles 89

Odd 91

One Mic 95

Royal 99

Six Strings 100

Soldiers 102

The Storm 106

Til The Time 109

Underneath 111

Unexpected 115

Walking With No Reason 118

Why? 121

You Served Your Purpose 122

LIFE LESSONS **125**

A Letter To My Mother 126

Accepted 129

Be Loved 132

Behind The Glasses 137

Black 139

Blood 142

Broken Mirrors 144

Clean Record 145

Drill 147

Family Controversy 149

Flow 151

I Couldn't Be Even More Proud 156

I Love Myself 159

I Wish 162

I'm A Winner 164

I'm Different 166

I'm From 168

In This Moment 172

Inner Self 175

It's Just Around The Corner 177

Life 179

Lights 181

Motivation 185

My Letter To My Father 188

New Beginning 191

Survival 194

Title 197

None Since 199

On My Block 202

Open Ears 205

Scream 208

Shadow 211

Stand Up 213

Starving 215

The Norm 219

The Road 222

Them Peaceful Waters 225

This Could Be My Last 229

Thug Rain 232

Time 235

Times Change.. 239

Unfriended... 242

Unwanted 244

We're No Different 246

Welcome.. 249

White Child 251

Who Are You? 253

TALKING THAT SPIRITUAL 254

Bending Knees 255

GO In God's Peace 259

Healed.. 261

I'm Blessed 263

In The Mix Of It All 268

One Word Away.. 270

Pure... 277

Reborn 280

Step Aside 281

Surrender 283

ABOUT THE AUTHOR...................................289

LOVE VS. LUST

I'll Wait For You

See the truth is I'm not in a relationship

I kept it that way for a while

Just to wait on that one person that is worth the while

Now I am not looking for a one night

Somebody who does not fit my type

Just the one person who will be honored to be my wife

Yes

I said honored

There are LOTS of fine women out here

I am not starving from hunger

There are so many fishes in the sea who will be great for me

I am not falling for games

So

She could take from me

Yes

As the older men would say

"She got skin, and really looks good"

I stopped eating pork
I am barely looking for women in the hood

Do not get me wrong
I am all about true love
My generation barely knows anything about that

They are looking for a nice body
Nice face
Has that good-good

Sorry to say
That is why so many young women get popped at a young age
I mean knocked up

We as men got them words
That makes women heat up

So

I'll cool down

Wait for her

Whoever she may be

I'll just know she will be a gift from Jesus for me

She will be my Goddess and I'll be her God

We will love each other so much

That we share the same heart

Yes

I'll wait for the one who makes us a union

One body

If it is true love

There will be no need to cheat with nobody else

I'll love you as you love me back

No matter the differences or issues we may have down the line

I'll find a lady who is somebody

Someone I'll be honored to say I waited for

A woman I am not afraid to say she is mine

Until then

I'll wait for you

Yes

I'll wait for you

I'm Not Afraid

I'm not afraid to change my ways

If it means

You'll love me always

I'll say I love you all day

Just looking in your eyes takes my breath

I know

Deep in my soul our love shall never get old

So no

I'm not afraid

To show how much I love you

Even if I must publicly kiss you on a CTA blue line train

All eyes on us

Our heat turned into a fire

I can turn it higher

Next stop it's whatever you desire

In the cut

That's where we burn

Hoping another train Isn't coming

Now it's your turn

I'm not afraid

To go all day

Saying I love you
Putting kisses all over your face
knowing we in that mood
Some things we want to do

We can wait

Take things slow
But just know
I'm not afraid
I am not
afraid

I'm So Into You

I watch from a far

As your glamorous shine in the light

Protecting you and watch closely for I want to be your knight

Your knight in shining armor

Doing all the makes you happy

Fighting in your honor

I watch from a far as you dance around the room

Hoping you will spin my way

As you fall in my arms and we dance the night away

I watch from a far

For I'm so into you

There are so many fine women out tonight

No one compares to you

I'm so into you

From your personality

That smile

The way you are so natural and real

I wonder if you know how I really feel

You started a conversation

I once done the same

Just hearing my name from your lips is like a trip to paradise and back

I'm so into you

I'll do anything to prove it to you

We are friends for now

I just want you to understand that I want to be more

Do more

For you are my Goddess in your riches and poor

I just want the opportunity to love you more

For I'm so into you

Yes

I'm so into you

I cannot see my life without you

Without needing you

Can I please you and do your every desire

For whatever you need is my desire

As I watch from a far

Speak from my heart

I'm just hoping

We could take our friendship just a little more far

Just Once

In the clear eyesight of thou

And

Still invisible

I'm a none factor to thou
Thee shadow in me
Was my only hope for something
Someone

To see me

Thou didn't acknowledge me
Thou didn't see me
I'm unknown to thee
Not thou savior
Thou who lives

And

Breathe

My same air

Can thou just once feel my presence

Hear my voice

Touch me with care

As if love wasn't a choice

I put my breath on hold

Just to see if I still exist

Turning purple in the face

My feelings finally match my headache

Nearly passed out

Because

I lost my breath pace

Just once can thou speak to me

I seek to be a person that's notice

A person that's known

Don't have to be famous

But that

Knock on the door for somebody is looking for me

Just once can somebody tell me they care

To know we'll make it through this struggle for life isn't fair

Just once I want to be held

For a person to lift me up after I fell

Just once can thou make me feel like I'm somebody

I might be independent

Blessed with money and things

But

To know somebody have you for life means everything

Just once

Is this too much to ask?

You can show love unto me then leave it in the past

For love

Happiness

And

Joy seem as it wasn't meant to last

I ask just for once

Just once

Lost In Time

I see a girl
She looks so fine
Everything you could think of

Yeah

This girl is a dime

Nice personality
Educated
Independent
Great conversation
I didn't even have to spend it

Yeah look at me

Started dating before I was a teen
Had me a few girls while I was still in grammar school
Who would've known that a church boy like me would have girls?

What in the world was I thinking?
Relationship moving too fast
What was you drinking?

Young and lost that was me
Some girl I've dated tried to take advantage of me
I couldn't believe it

Classroom closet
That's where it gone down
Girls in middle school getting talked into pulling their pants down

Never forget that quiet sound

My homies in the closet with a female on her knees

With her hands down

Too much of a church boy I didn't mind being
Knowing what's going on without seeing
There was no forcing me to being
"The man"

I was a child
Didn't want that chance
Didn't understand
Like as soon as y'all made 13
Y'all was happy y'all friend can spit

I didn't get it

So lost in time

What happen to talking?

Hoping a date you'll find

Carrying protection until the right time

As for me

I was

lost

in

time

Nerd

What's good nerd?

I heard you was smart

Love to learn

Has a big heart

Hay nerd

You're not fooling me

Of course

You're smart as ever

Not the person people thinking you'll be

A yo nerd

I saw you at that party talking to some girl and disrespecting somebody

Hallo nerd

You're not tricking me

You're single

I'm single

This the perfect place to be

Hi nerd

I heard you don't have a man

Been in one heart breaking relationship
Now you're afraid to give the next guy a chance

Nerd you're beautiful
I could be wasting my time on females that all the guys want
Trying to have something with you
I feel all my time is useful

You hide your true self under what people portray you to be
I'm looking pass how you nerd yourself down

I know you're into me
Just don't what to be down

So

Nerd

If you're looking for a relationship or anything

I'll be around

Paradise

Come with me to see how beautiful thee are
For thee are my Goddess
In thou my lover I found peace

I love her
Thou are a sight to see
Men nude eyes

Worth living for
In darkness your beauty still shines
Thou are mine

I love thee
My flesh reunites with hers
We will stay together for infinity

Thou are my sources
Thou are my being
Whom I am addressing?

Whom I am seeing?
Paradise
What a beautiful name

My love

Beautiful is thou

For beautiful things flows within thee

I always love seeing the visual

The way we laid in grass

Watching the air blow through her hair

Her natural of nature fills my space

Paradise

Thou are everywhere

To be with thee

Lost in her rainforest

Covering myself with her leaf

I love the way thou refresh me

Paradise

I love thee

Getting lost in her jungle

Only surviving off thee

You my love

Paradise

You look so good to me

I could be homeless

Yet I survive off her Earthly sources
In you paradise
Thou are my life

For thee lives in me

She Loves Me, She Loves Me Not

Beautiful as a sunflower

Sharp as a thorn

I pick at you like a red rose

Your attitude is like a dandelion

Gone with the wind

Where should I begin?

She loves me

She loves me not

Something like hugging a cactus without a drink of a shot

Pretty as a blossom on a sunny day

Blooms into cute colorful flowers

Until it falls in Fall

Slowly Winter is coming

You're not that beautiful at all

She loves me

She loves me not

Like a Leif that falls from the tree and blows in natural air
As she whispers in my ears softly and leaves me there

The fresh smell of flowers as she walks pass
Feeling the room up with her fresh wash hair that's smells like cut pine
wood
Made into a shank

We sit on shore and watch the ocean line up with the skyline
As the sun goes down
So beautiful

I wish it was

Spending time with her could be like watching a swamp

She loves me

She loves me not

I think of her nonstop
She opens her heart and I fell in her flytrap
Swallowing me down venous got me trapped

Glamorous as a shining diamond found in an open field

Gorgeous as butterflies showing their true colors inside the greenhouse

I pull a pink rose out the ground
No matter what happens I'll still love you
For she loves me

She loves me not

She loves me

She loves me not

I thought I was done

I see one under my thumb

Can't believe it

She loves me

The Walk

Let's take a stroll in each other's life

Taking the journey through love and fights

Is it alright to spend the night in each other's hearts?

I'll like to stay there even when it gets hard

Life is hard

Going to continue to be that way

You'll be royalty if you walk my way

Can we at least try?

Shoot our shots

See how far we may go

Promise me through the journey you won't let go

Let's take a stroll

Call it the walks of life

For in every relationship there'll be a fight

I'll be afraid if you walk out my life

What's Love?

What's love?

What's trust?

What's loyalty?

What's understanding?

What's commitment?

What's faithful?

What's honesty?

What's love?
Is it deep felt or just a feeling?
Does it require emotions or just motions?
Like when the boat moves inside your ocean
Makes you feel like Earth, Wind, and Fire you give devotion

What's trust?
Is it being trustworthy or being worthy to be trust?
Like when you say you love another person

But

Deep inside you just want her cherry to bust
His condom to break for that's not love
Only a feeling that couldn't wait

What's loyalty?
Is it being loyal or just seeking to putting the work in?
Receive his or her royalty
Just hoping to burst
Can't hold it in any longer you've erupted fireworks

What's understanding?

Because

Xscape need it
Trying to create a relationship

But

That one person just wants you to speed it
Sorry to say
Your body that boy or girl need it

What's commitment?
Is it to be committed?

Saying I do

Or

Your mind deep in the pants and you're thinking I'll do anything for you

What's faithful?
Is it base off faith?
You're supposed to wait until you get married

Of course

Your hormones can't wait

So

 I

Say

What's honesty?
Is it being honest to another person and telling the truth?

Or

You hooked on Phonics like Ebonics and like to have fun with the lights
out

What's that about?

There is a difference you know

Love is love and sex is sex

Yes

Love and sex are a beautiful thing
That happen alone with being in love
It's deeper

Heartfelt

Soul felt

To show emotions

To say I love you

To say I care

Stop getting confused with what's in your underwear

If you truly love a person

If you want to create a bond

Trust

Honesty

Loyalty

Commitment

A faithful relationship

Then of course your every desire will be there

THINKING OUT LOUD

12 Years Straight

12 years straight

I've been bullied and picked on

12 years straight

My emotions been spitted and stepped on

12 years straight

I been used and back stabbed

12 years straight

Just to be cool I had to be fake

Just to find out I'm the one most people hated

12 years straight

I been the crow

Not even counting birth

That's more things I don't want to think about

Due to the hurt

I live my life

My soul will shine through the broken cracks of my heart

Them 12 years

I'm talking about my education

Just to go through all that pain so it could one day reach the nation

12 years straight

37

YEAH

I've endured some pain

Sorry for what happen to the ones in the process

12 years straight

I've been bullied and picked on

Who would've thought I'll be the one you all depend on?

Four Walls

I sit in my room

Looking at the wall

Mind completely gone

No thoughts at all

I began to rock

Rock back and forward

Door closed wondering what I'm sitting for

I lay back

Lay back in my bed

Just lying there freely in my underwear

Window open

So

I feel the air

It's blazing hot and I'm just there

In my bed sweat running down my body as I inhale and exhale

Boxed in my room four walls

I close my eyes and thoughts began to come

One man and two guns

My imagination has begun

One team

Five bats

That is how it feels when I am being disrespected
My mind disconnected as I started to blink
The lights hit my eyes as I jumped up

Mind too clear

Somebody about to get fucked up
Hardcore people can only be hard core once they step up

I stand up
Began to pace
Walking back and forward on the floor of faces I hate

I am sorry for I do not even have the pictures
You can imagine my anger
If you visualize the picture
Boxed in my room four walls
Have thoughts that I shouldn't be thinking at all
Even a positive child has a point when they would fall
Surrounded by these four walls

I refuse to go out

Trying to be humbled

Get all this negative out my mind and mouth

In my bedroom boxed in these four walls

I learned to be humbled and keep my cool

No telling what I would have done to you

I sit on the edge of my bed

Remembering how much I love you

Began to smile never forgetting how much I need you

We gone through a lot that will make me hate you

Spending time within these four walls

I started to think how I will be without you

A Dream

I have done my best
That was all I can do

I just cannot

What you want me to do listen?

Lean on your every word?

I have a mind of my own

This is my life

I live it however I feel

Let me be the crow
At least I would have learned how to survive on my own

The path waited for whom fell for it

I have slipped through the cracks of shaking grounds
Roses would not be beautiful until it gone through dirt
Showered down your experience

Your truth

The sun did not shine

SO

Why am I the shadow behind you?

I would have looked up to you

I would have let you lead

BUT

I am dying of life
No mud found
No soil either

I needed to rise
Rise like the sun in the Summertime
Just so ever shined
Looked for leadership in that seed that died
Might be a crow

BUT

I used to fly

How dare you talked death upon me

I have survived

No more sleeping

 I have arisen

Am I My Brother's Keeper?

There is a question about my loyalty

My brotherhood

My manhood

Am I My brother's keeper?

Am I loyal?

Am I all about brotherhood?

Can I stay true to my man hood?

Am I my brother's keeper?
That is a question I never understood
How could you trust a person who will smile in your face?
Once you do something that they do not approve
There is something smart to say

Am I my brother's keeper?
How could you ask?
All I have done was be true to myself and others
Yet get stabbed in the back

Am I my brother's keeper?
Why would you even question that?
I am the one who is all for the cause
Deep in my brotherhood

Am I my brother's keeper?
What make you question my manhood?
All men have soft ways
Just won't show them

Am I my brother's keeper?
Do not call me your brother

Shit

We are not even homies
That is crazy

Am I my brother's keeper?
I wonder why I even dealt with you

Am I my brother's keeper?
Only to a very few
Do not ask me anymore questions
I do not fuck with you

Appreciated

Don't ask no questions

Just go with it

Just laughed and smile

Then leave me alone

I apologize

That's how I am

Don't talk to me

Don't touch me

Until it's time

I love you all to death and after

You all generosity is not what I'm after

I'm like a picture painted with no capture

Just to be noticed is enough

I'm nice once all eyes on me

I'm also the black sheep

I know you all are phony

Maybe it's just me

I wasn't getting a lot of attention

I really love and appreciate my siblings

Nieces

Nephew

Paint the picture

Six nieces

Three sisters

Two brothers

One nephew

One child on the way from one of my sisters

I'm petty and rude to all of them in my own ways

Yet

Appreciate them all
They're the reason I'm the person I am today
I appreciate them so much
They know it
I'm lost in the mind

They're not afraid to show emotions

I'm lost

It's like I'm soft

Sentimental too

Rude and petty all at the same time

Maybe because I was treated like a child for a long time

Spoil

Sweet

Having to not barely fight
My siblings defended me
Took up for me
Barely got into anything
Appreciated
That's what you all are
To have a group of people
Family
To have your back no matter what happens
Is like trying to tell Captain Crunch he ain't the captain

So

To my siblings

Nieces

Nephew

You all are so appreciated
No matter what I say and do
You all are so appreciated

Honored

Loved

So

Appreciated
Despite what I'll say
It is because of all of you
I'm the person I am today

(Look for part two coming soon)

Brighter Days

The beginning of the chapter wasn't always once upon a time
This nonfiction

The painted picture that has been seen
Only mix chemicals with lies in the mixture

Let me borrow the paintbrush
No need for water mixed colors

You blend and I turn
I am original

Proud of the richness
The fruits so pure

How could you let me rot?
when you use my resources

Let me paint the picture
You let it dry

The image so deep
Do not close your eyes

It is funny

How I shine through your darkness

Color me bad

I do not want to sex you up

The lies you told

Somebody going to get you fucked up

With a hard-long truth

Stop fucking lying to motherfuckers

We are all beautiful

No matter if we are light skin

Dark skin

Shit even mixed racial

Stop fucking belittling people

Paint the picture

Tell the stories behind them

DNA cannot tell us apart from the roots

Trying to deny when we pump the same blood

The stories are just the end

When it could have been a happy ever after

Don't

I don't need the money

Clothes

Fame

That's going to come anyway

Don't try to put me on with no girls

Your ex's

 I need a lady

Who is going to stand by my side?
 No matter what happens

Please don't

Does it look like I need friends?

A group of users and takers
Don't give a fuck about me
Talking behind my back

Acting like I'm slow and shit

You all are around me everyday
 There's no reason to be so geek to see me like that

Oh

Yeah

That's that phony shit

Just cool with me so I can support bad habits

What I need is a word from the Lord
Somebody who love me either rich or poor
He opened doors

So

I can open doors for others

Even the ones that disrespect me
I still love them like a brother

It's powerful how many tongues are used
To put people down
The same tongues will thank you

Say they love you

Like I said

That's that phony shit

As much as I want to hate you all

Say fuck all of you motherfuckers

I see myself inside of each of you

Electronic

Times change

Things got easier

Phones

Tablets

Laptops and more

All you ever wanted to know and do is all in your fingertips

All in the control of your hands

So easy

Fast

Simple

You barely need a human

Electronics

What a powerful addiction

The new ruler of the mind

Stuck in technology

Apps and data that your mind you can't find

So easy that we as humans got lazy

So fast that we dummy down

Isn't that something?

Shorten the words

Made the language emojies

But

We're addicted

I AM

I take pride in myself for I am what I am

No need to change

I am the source of all being
The reason your seeing
The reason your breathing
The energy you need to do anything

I am the created

I am the Earth
No need to hide it

I will not deny it
All I am not doing is fighting it

I am the known and unknown
Just like you see me and now you do not

I am the making and the dead
With skills you once had

I am the now that you will see later

You will not understand if you are a hater

I am the truth and the light
The darkness at night

I am an image out of sight
Powerful then a dynamite
So weak

I would not put up a fight

I am you and you are me
All you see is a human being

I am the flesh and the soul

I am young and old
I told you before I am Earth
From the dirt to the sky no questions why
I have died already

Now I am back alive

I am not Jesus

I am God made in his image

So

I am a creator

No need to praise me or thank me
Everything made me what I am now

For

I

Am

A vision inside your dream

The cameras that shoot the scenes

The one you cannot define

Because

I am everything

Like

Everything

I am the person

Place

And

Thing

Yes

 Just like a noun

Can you hear me now?

These words hurt more than me being a verb

And

Taking actions

I

Am

The bad and good

Like coming from church to the hood

So

Am I more Christian?

Or

More Thug?

Either way I still need love
That hug
Tell me you care more than enough

I am not soft

But

I am not tough

Just keep praying and thinking about me for this pain is too much

For

I

Am

Your smile you hide under tears

Killing you softly

You kept in all these years

I am your drug and beer

Thinking about the old times

Wishing that one person was still here

I am that happiness and joy

When you cannot stop smiling for what God has in storage

Keep thanking him for opening doors

Screaming

I

Will

Praise

You

Forever more

I am what I am

I am not running

I am not hiding

I am standing out

Showing out

Because

You will know what I am about

And

Who

I

Am

I Just Want To Express Myself

Who you are to judge me?

Did you buy anything I have on?

Who you are to tell me what and what not to say?

These are my lips and I say what I want

I say what I mean

I mean what I said

If you do not like it

To fucking bad

Who are you to tell me how to act?

I stay true to myself no matter where I am at

I am not going to pretend and listen to you

Think back

Back in the days

Right?

When you were acting wild and doing whatever you liked

Trying to put the blame on me and my generation

Nah

You all are not getting off that easy

You all started some of the things we do

Keep talking that good stuff

Now let's look at you all

Simple as this everything coming back in style

From what you all generation done

What can I say?

You all dropped the ball

Then some stop caring

We are the reflection of the past generation

Just like they are the reflection of the ones before them

Where the leadership gone?

What happen to the generosity?

I might not know everything

Yet

I do not see the legacy that was left for my generation

You all have so much to say

I do not see no hands that is helping

Be quick to pick up the phone or report some shit

On the generation that you all dropped the ball on

So quick to talk down on us

When we have the chance to express ourselves

Awe

Now it is nothing you all want to discuss

It pisses me off how you all stop caring

Now the generation you all talk bad about

You all are burying

Not saying there is no leaders

Not saying there is no good people out here

Shit

I just wish it would be more

How could you judge us all?

When some of us are trying our best

Do not keep judging me

I just want to express myself

I Just Want To Make You Proud

To whom it may concern

I was wrong

Speaking encouragement

I am the same person who stoned you

I was wrong

All you wanted to do was to make it big in life

You ask for my help

I told you to have a nice life

How could I be so bold

Telling you the same things I have been told

How could I be so bold

You extended your hand

My pride did not let me reach out to hold

You saw greatness

A bright future in me

All the pain I have cause you

I hope you can see that there was

Evilness within me

You are my mentor
You are my friend

You are my leader
I will follow until the end

There is no replacing you
Only facing you

All I have done
I am proud of you

I just want to make you proud
I am not looking for forgiveness

Not even your friendship
I do not deserve that

To make you proud of me
Yourself

We both done damage
We both deserve to smile again

I was wrong

You were wrong

Two powerful people spitting on each other thrown
I just want to make you proud

We both build that thrown
I just want to make you proud

We stand together

Or

On

Our

Own

I Rise

Like the sun in the morning

I rise

Shining brightly in the peep of my eyes

I rise

Like water tides

My life is the waves lifted from the wind

So

I'll keep rising

Water

Air

Never ends

Been knocked down on my butt

So

I'll sit on a chair

Hands touch the chair legs

I've been lifted in the air

Even when I'm down I still rise

Like a roller coaster at the carnival

Six flags

I rise at the peak until the drop

I'll keep rising

The ride hasn't stop

Like a balloon filled with oxygen that's let go by a child

I rise high in the sky until the human eyes can't see me

I rise

Continually move ahead

If you keep going backwards

You will end up dead

So

I rise

Yes

I rise

I'm Sorry

Is this the right time for me to apologize?
When all you tried to do was help me in life

Open my eyes

Clear my mind

Negative should be out my head
It is time to think positive this time

Chances after chances
Opportunities never looked so possible in my eyes

My brain was fried

I have never been on drugs
I only smoked a lot of weed

Running for baptism
The demon that was in me had ambition

I apologize

I failed the mission

Giving a simple test

I did not listen

Did not obey
Did not pass the test

I apologize for my words

What the hell do I need you for?

Yes

You helped
You opened doors

It has been years after years
I am still poor

Help was needed

Help took a long ass time to complete

Trying to smile in your generosity
When what I really wanted to do was grind my teeth

I apologize

OR

Should I say I am sorry?

Sorry means until the next time
The next time I hope I will be treated better

So

Nothing would not happen like the last time

I feel blue
I am spitting rhymes

Trying to show my appreciation
While speaking my mind

I am grateful
Thankful too

BUT

Life is short

I am sorry

I'm Not Perfect

I'm not perfect
Not trying to be

People love to judge

All in the next person business

Wonder why I'm so mental

Over judging

First impression
Love the way I have people guessing

Love dressing
Joking

Acting a fool

I'm a church boy
Human too

Very handsome
I may even look good

I'm not perfect
I'm a decent person

Can hang with anybody

Do what you do
I'm not going to tell nobody

I'm not perfect
I know where I stand

I'm not a thug
You won't see a 30 in my hand

There's no bags of loud on me
People hardcore life don't move me

I'm not perfect
Just being myself

Like what I like

I'm not perfect
Just love having fun

Hanging out

Trying new things
Traveling and exploring

I'm not perfect
Don't like to be bored

I do whatever I want
Without being force

That's how I feel

I'm not perfect

Just feel how I feel
One thing for sure

I'm a truthful person

I'm not perfect
I keep it real

Journey

I sit at the window

Just sitting there and relaxing

Watching a part of the world go past and wondering what will happen

What will I see?

Who will I meet?

What will I eat?

I take the ride

Just speeding through towns

Stopping at different locations as I hear the whistle sound

I stare out the window

Glancing at the views

So many beautiful sights

I only captured a few

I capture moments

Chills comes to my flesh as I cover my body with a hoodie

Becoming warm

I sit by the window

Just looking at land

Grass

Trees

Water

Crops

Will it ever end?

I see animals
They are at peace

Cows

Horses

Pigs

Roosters

Flock of birds flying out of the pond

My thoughts begun
I knew I was not sleep after seeing mudslides

Ditches

Creeks

81

I sit by the window and remember I am no longer in Chicago
I left some hours ago
No wonder why I felt slow as I joke

I mean this ride is fast but long
I am keep forgetting I am traveling to my father's home

Laughing

Talk what you know
Not what you heard

Say what you mean
What you have seen

You are trying to expose me
To make yourself feel better

I know I am not perfect
I have done some things

I am human

Let's Take A Trip

A child been killed

Children have goals and dreams

A teen been shot

Teenagers have goals and dreams to accomplish

A young adult been murdered

Young adults have their lives to live

Let's take a trip

Let's take a trip in your mind

Every time something happens that's violent and wrong

We're on every News channel when you turn your television on

Making lies

Hiding the truth

How would you feel if the breaking News headline was you?

I'm exploring your mind

Only negative things are what I found

You call us all thugs and gang bangers
Just preparing for the worst

I see graduates who's succeeding
Putting negative people like you in your place

Two places we once were told we'll be

Dead

Or

In jail

Yet

We have jobs

Receiving college degrees after college degrees
Focusing on our careers

Making our dreams into realities

My trip almost over
You have a headache?

Well

I'm going to keep speaking positive things until your skull breaks

Why the media don't showcase or talk about all the positive things we're
doing and done?
Hiding our accomplishments and achievements until the point nobody
on top

Let's take a trip

So

We can find out how bad you are tripping

How you going to tell a story when our info you missing?

You lying piece of shit

We are not what the media portray us to be

When I turn my television on
Our accomplishments and achievements are barely shown

When will you tell a truthful story and move the hell on?

MY Story

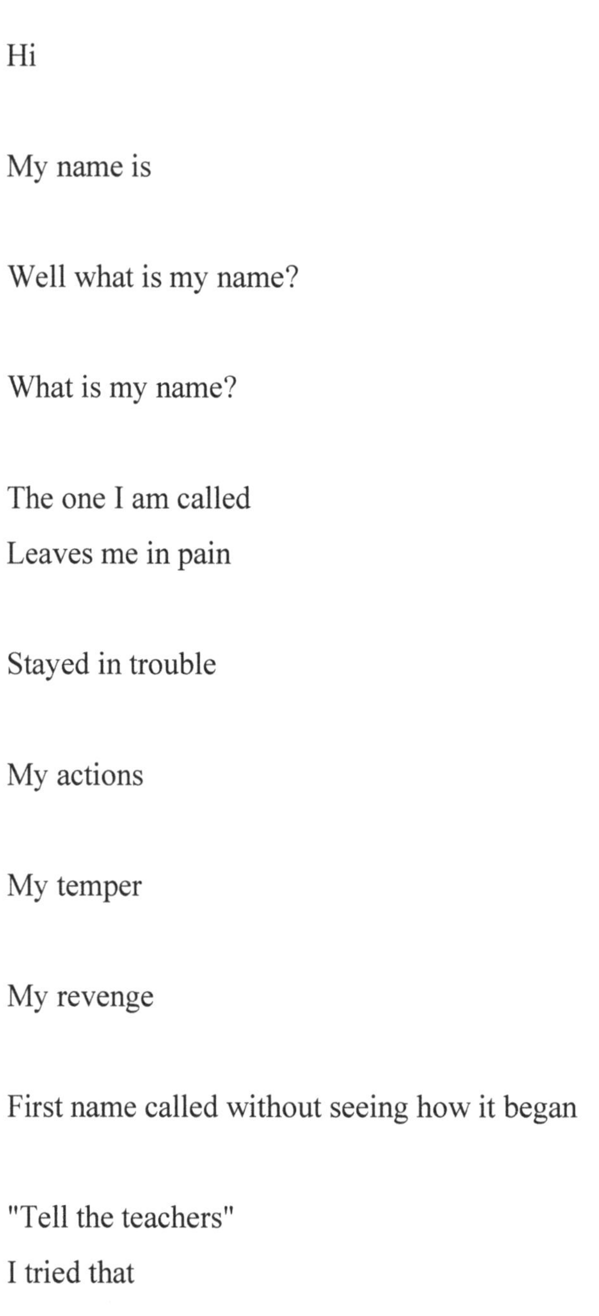

Hi

My name is

Well what is my name?

What is my name?

The one I am called
Leaves me in pain

Stayed in trouble

My actions

My temper

My revenge

First name called without seeing how it began

"Tell the teachers"
I tried that

Alone with other staffs

I ended up telling my mother
I am not trying to go down her same path

"Do what you have to do"

Fighting was not my intentions
Stayed getting bullied

I am the King of detentions
Never got suspended

So many knew what I was going through
Leading up to high school

My mother held me through

She said

"Never be afraid to tell me what's going on with you"

My parents alone with my sisters and brothers always confused me
First cool me down then ready to go fight somebody

Believe it or not
I barely fought people

Me being bullied all the time
I became known throughout grammar school

Middle school

High school

For just being me
Entertaining people while trying to be friendly

My name

My name

What is my name?

There is too many
It is hard to explain

Just

It is a story
Without the name

My Turtles

What are you all thinking?

How are you all feeling?

Can you all understand me?

Can you all hear me?

I know you all see me

Do you all like

Do you all like the way you all are being treated?

I barely see you all like that

I will make sure you all eat and clean

I mean I order and buy up to 500 to 1001 mealworms

All of them would be alive

Sun dried dead shrimp man that smells

I will do anything just so you all stay healthy and alive

I love my turtles

No matter what they do

Keep surviving

I love taking care of you all

Making sure nobody eats you all

Odd

Is it me or is it this world?

I do not understand the plan that is in the government hands

I have a master plan

To follow Jesus until the point he calls me home to Christ

For I have done my job

It was not for me to understand

Just seek Jesus first and put everything in his hands

The world is so odd

So

I'll lean on your words

Keep the faith

Never let go

It feels like sometimes my being is not meant to be a human being

Overseeing the truth

The light for this world

Was not meant for men and women

Build on numbers

Odd

We the people of the United States and other countries are not the people

Just numbers and papers

If you put all of us together

We are not equal

Odd

For the "People" who we claim to be are killing and destroying each

other lives

That is our history

Do not matter about your nationality

This is bigger than a race thing

My eyes have seen the set up the government has done

Odd

It is nothing wrong with government help

I am not lazy

It feels like I need to depend on the government to lend

I will just depend on my hands and knees

My Lord and Savior supplies all my needs

I am not lazy

That is what the world wants

Odd

It was not our plan to hustle and grind on streets

It is their plan so they could put us away in jail
For something they provided for us to fail

Odd

Schools are closing and new jails are built
People in service tilting off shots that was not communion
Their plan was to put liquor stores on the same corners or streets as
church's

Odd

It is hard to learn
They got rid of the good teachers
Just to hire the ones who do not care
In it for their tax returns
We are being trick

Yes

We need money for most things
I am not letting paper get inside my head to the point I am brain dead
and blinded to the rule of all evil

I know

I might have said too much

Some things you are not going to agree with

Just open your eyes

Understand when you wake up

94

This

is

Reality

One Mic

Is it my turn to speak?
Say a few thoughts

OR

Since this is my generation
I cannot get my point across

Stop judging me from what you see and hear on social media
You need to get some glasses

Clean out your ears

Focus on the positive that you do not even hear

Your mind so gone
People like me disappear

What happen?

Life use to be good

I mean going places with no worries

BUT

Now my generation want to carry guns
Where the hell you all bravery was at when our people was getting
hung?

All I need is one mic
To tell my generation that it is going to be alright

BUT

Do the media show my generation striving?
Do the media show my generation making our goals possible?

BARELY

YET

We are expected to be dumb founded
To be brainwashed

Blinded to lifestyles
Opportunities that few people from the hood gets

All I need is one mic
To tell my generation

The upcoming generation
Even the older generation that we must fight

Not like a war

BUT

That one day we all could put the guns down
Fight on these issues with the government

Where is our money going besides in jails and fighting the war?

All I need is one mic
To tell you why we so violent and heartless

We were looking for a light in all this darkness
That one chance to shine

Hearing I love you
To hear we are going to be fine

I am just one person trying to talk about our struggle
Our pain

Praying that we all can come together
Praying everything will be alright

BUT

All

I am

Asking for

Is

One

Mic

Royal

Look me in the eyes

Tell me what you see

When I stare in the mirror

I see royalty

A young King

Deep in the roots

I am a King

I am royalty

Just check the history

I am powerful

Honored

Respected in all ways

Feeling like a spade

Batter watch your hand

I am also an Ace in demand

Call it playing cards

The way I change faces

(Look for part two coming soon)

Six Strings

I hear a song

It sounds so beautiful
Touching I may say

The best performance I saw all day
The music moved me
The voice reached me

Only if I had the money to give
The pick struck the guitar
The lyrics flowed out the lips
Collecting cash

The talents painted a masterpiece of help and pain
Only if I had something to give
The sound of music of if he played on Broadway
Telling a story that connect with my dreams
He played melodies

I was drawn to his stories
Collect that money
Boy you batter collect
Pouring your soul out on this platform

He could've been in need

Maybe just wanted to be known

Receiving money in a good way

There's no need for begging

His songs were even positive

Yet so many misjudged him

He just asked for help when

He

Struck his six strings

Soldiers

I salute you my brothers

I salute you my sisters

No one could have done what you all done

I salute the soldiers
The veterans
Fighting the war
Protecting us

I salute the daily soldiers
Dealing with daily life
The ones who struggle just to provide
The ones who go out their ways

Just

So

We

Can

Stay

Alive

Realize that in life we must do all that is necessary
Just so we can survive

"I love the way you fight"

I once told that to my mother
Bad situation
She might did not hear the right information
Not violent

But

As a mother helping to supply
Give your tides to six children

Talk about trying to meet the Brady Bunch needs

My father done all he can as well
Footlocker shoes and all
Seem like my parents is giants
It's hard to see them fall

I salute the ones who is living a hood life

A street life

People misjudged you all

Keep the grind right
Keeps the families tight

I salute the ones that is living in the suburbs

The ones in the projects
I am originally from

Yes

Our

Lives

Are

Hard

It feels like it is over

But

We won

We are not dead
It is only beginning

To all the soldiers
Struggling or not
You are all loved
Appreciated

Honored
No one could do what you all are doing
What you all have done
There is no one who could fill you all spots

The Storm

Last night I cried the tears of rain drops

Falling so cold on the living and dead

For I am the reason beautiful things comes out my pain

Hoping it rain for my tears is full of pollution

The ones who made the lighting come out of me

Just hoping not to electrocute the ones I've put energy into

It's sad how I can make everything so beautiful

Sunny

Green

Until somebody does the wrong things to me

Now every living thing is running

For the forecast said there's a storm on the way

Sad to say

There's no coverage

There's a price to pay

The storm is on the way

Not knowing how I'm going to come

So be prepared for everything

I could turn into anything

Right now

I'm just going to shower down the pain I've Endured

Until the clouds come down and things look blur

I think about the pollution

My eyes form the drizzle

Knowing I've been hurt more than a little

Tears picking up as I rain my face out

Trying to stop before I flood this Earth out

The wind gets heavy blowing things around

Blowing quietly forming a mass destruction of spinning objects in the air

Just by me breathing so hard

Taking deep breaths

Trying to easy it out my nose slowly

The times I've yelled shaking the sky in anger with my voice

The clouds felt me go through them like a lighting ball

Making points on objects as people crawl to hide

The image of my pain

Struggles

And

Anger is very disturbing

My mind is a light switch

You only get two sides of me

All in the finger of your flick

Like your fuel to my Bic

Strike your thumb down my back one time

You really going to find out the saying "I'm burning" means

For my heart is burning in anger

When the ones you love treats you like a stranger

Brings all your hopes and dreams down and toss you on a hanger

Just leave you there to dry

No need to cry for help now

For I'm not the storm that comes and mess up everything

I'm the one who's there to help you in your storms

Telling you to have faith

To move on

But

If you mess over me

The other side of me will be reborn

Til The Time

Sitting on the tip of the bed looking at the wall

Barely blinking

Body so still

Thoughts so clear

Like a person at rest

Mind gone

Blood still flows

Hearing air through my nose

As I inhale deeply

Exhale slow

Thinking in my mind what's life for

Nineteen years straight none stop

Dealing with pain as a tear dropped

Name callings

Being bully is a daily activity

Just waiting til the time it's all over

Take it how you want to

Dead or alive

At this point even I don't know why I'm alive

For I have yet to live my life

Finished twelve years of being educated

Thirteen if you count head start

Even graduated with honors

It feels like I'm not a star

Til the time comes it's going to always feel like I've done what's
expected

How I'm supposed to feel when all this time I've been mentally and
emotionally damaged?

Without being protected

Til the time comes I'm going to do some messed up things and even
explore

Until I find out what's life worth living for

To do my own things

I'm not label rich or poor

Til the time

I'm going to suffer

Live til the time

I find out what's life has in storage for me

Underneath

Ever thought why I am so mean?

Why I am so cruel?

Why I am real petty?

Why I do not give a you know what?

Why do you think I act this way?

What makes you think underneath is just play?

I like jokes though
I lost my childhood
A long way somewhere
You all took care of me
Does not mean you all was there
Barely listened to me

I am sorry

You all were not there
Everybody done their parts
That is a sign of not caring

Just make sure I develop into a young man
Graduate high school

Right?

Only if you all knew how I felt some nights
Things happened
I cannot make right

Well

While I am clearing my mind
I got addicted to somethings
Then I stopped
I started hanging with people
Asking myself why they are hiding from the cops
That really was not for me either

So

I stopped

Only if you all knew how I felt underneath my secret life
Me trying to stay church like
Knowing damn well I was not right
Not saying I do not believe
I very so do

Just

Read between the lines
I am still trying to find the person I was meant to be
People kept bugging
Wanting to know a little about me
I do not believe in being judged

Shit

We all made mistakes
Just
Follow your heart
Go for your dreams
That is what I would have told myself
Only if I was me

Underneath I tried to do right
Tried to make a bond
It was like I was loved deeply

But

Slipped from you all arms
I am not mean
I am not cruel

Just hoping

Once you all put two and two together

I

Will

Still

Be

Loved

Underneath you all cracked hearts

Unexpected

Look at me

Just look at me

I've been highly favored

While barely making a living

Barely surviving

Got a taste of the real life

It feels like I'm dying

I guess you can say I'm heading down a path with no direction

So many dreams

Goals

Blessed with outstanding talents

Nowhere to go

It gets colder than you know

When your dreams you hold

Your life you decide to throw

Trying to make it big in life

When there's no effort to putting the work in

So

You think your future is over

When this is the time your career begins

Yes

I'm addressing myself
Alone with speaking in general
If you don't go after your dreams
Your goals
There will be soon a funeral
A funeral
Not for the flesh
For the soul
A funeral
Not for your dreams
For your goals
A funeral

We are killing the ones who could had more out of life
Forgetting about the ones who showed us the light
The ones who open their arms to us
Doors to Opportunities and chances
I didn't even know were possible

Just look at me
I've made things happened
That was unexpected
Moved so many people unexpected
For what I've expected

It made me suspect that I'll never get no respect

Every time I rise above the judgmental

Just look at me

All my achievements were unexpected in school and out

That just shows what I'm about

I've been honored

Success is my daily goals

Hopefully somebody would look at me

Someday I'll be even more successful than you ever expected

Walking With No Reason

Pushing people away

Don't have anything to say

Don't start a conversation

About how was my day

People are more important than you

Smile on my face

I joke around

Deep inside of my heart

There's an empty space

Loving while careless I'll say

Calling me names

I hope not to be one day

I have all control of my mind

Body

Soul

Continually drive that mind set into someone

Is your idea and how you wanted them to be

There's no secret about me being different

It wasn't meant for me to follow

To lead and oversee my people to victory

Even though some might talk down upon me

They see the fighter in me

Just wish they could be me

You can shadow

You can shine

I don't even know what path I'm going down

Help after help

Still a cold road

People in my life

Don't want me to succeed

Petty and rude you may say

A bird can't fly when it's wing is clinch

It feels like I want to take miles

You don't even provide an inch

So disrespectful

It's like I don't have a heart

Disconnected

We grew apart

Not knowing we'll need each other again

Despite our differences

There's a spark
In the blood that runs so cold
I bleed low blood pressure of veins that's frozen

I pressure that spark
To talk about things that no longer burns within me
What's the point of trying when people attention level is 0% toward you?
Young adult is the reason toward me
I'm the only one that sees the child in me

Why?

There was no freedom until my teen years
I'm still a teen hanging on to every word
Barely living my life or dreams
Times changed
Children been added
Pushing me away more
I'm more depressed

All I ever wanted was somebody to listen to me for once
Understand me
Hear a yes
Walking with no reason
No wonder I'm a mess

Why?

Why even bother the "Untouchables"?

The ones who plays around

Jokes around

Talking all this gang crap

Thinking they won't get shot down

I don't even gang bang

I'm not about that life either

I'm just trying to speak life into other lives

Hoping that someone gets the message

See the afterlife

You Served Your Purpose

I am done with this
All this fake hanging
Acting like we're cool
Once you get what you wanted
You're done with me

Until later or whenever

Yes

I been used

Serving you for whatever you need me to do
I'm through serving
I've served my purpose for the thought of you
Done whatever you told me to
I was the answers to you

Yes

I'm needed
Like your need to feed the urge of drugs you don't need
You need me
For I am your drugs you crave so deeply

Yes

I am your addiction
You're hungry

But

Nothing cooking in the kitchen

So

Listen you starving prick
The ways I been misused made me sick
You can play all you want until I put your ass on pause

Yes

I am your remote
I have all control to you troll
You evil doll
Try to use me again I'm ripping your ass apart
For your heart I thought was sweet and soft as cotton
Until you fucked over me and I ate you alive as if you were candy

Yes

I am your need

All you ever done to me

I'm just controlling you

Karma is a real bitch you haven't met yet

124

But

You will

LIFE LESSONS

A Letter To My Mother

Dear mother

How did you do it?
Bringing up six children who all need special attention

You are beautiful

Bold

Did I mention blessed?

You try your best and done all you can
I cannot speak for everybody

BUT

You are my mother and friend

Dear mother

I love you
I know I feel I do not need nobody

BUT

I will be lost without you

Sorry about all the times I have disrespected you
Finish high school

Get a job

Be who you were meant to be in life
While loving who you are

That was not much to ask out of me

BUT

Being under you a lot I did not know what or who I wanted to be
Just hoping whatever I become and do you will be proud of me

Dear mother

Life is not what it seems
Having a perfect family is only in movies and dreams

Having to learn about the hood life before I even made a teen
Words cannot express and tell how I really feel

You were always there for me

I cannot speak for everybody

I would not compare my mother to others

I just feel no one can compare to the things you have done

For this is my letter

My letter to my mother

Accepted

If I was a thug would you love me?

Some in the closet queer

Would you love me?

If I was poor would you help?

If I was rich would you be phony?

There is no life without struggling

Survival only

If I was smart would you care?

If I was dumb would you care?

Being educated and successful do not define me

If I was

What if I am

Does it matter?

Life is not an award

I am not getting my name on a plat

So

Either accept me or do not

If I was more Christian would you love me?
If I was Earthlier would you love me?
Either way I am still having to go through storms

Do you still love me?
Do you still care?
My life is my life

My decisions I will keep
This just the beginning
Who knows what is ahead of me?

I might adapt
I might explore
I might discover

Having fun

Wrong ways
Right ways
Is there a such thing?

I could have lack of knowledge
Force into some things
I may not know my path yet

So

Yes

I might be curious

I mean that in all ways
It does not have to mean that I am homosexual

Or
A straight up hardcore ride or die gang banger

But

I just might want to test the waters
If I was
Just if I became

Would you love or just accept me?
One thing for sure
Only life can change me

So

Accept me or do not
Somebody will

Be Loved

You not my type

I'm not attracted to you

I look at you like my brother

I think of you as my sister

You not this

You not that

You too this

You too that

Shit

I wonder why people stay single

Keep getting their hearts and feelings hurt

The shit funny to me

Only a few years ago you were once the ones you judge

Shit

Or will be

Now you have people all over you

Trying to get with you

Now you think you are the perfect dream

Watch out

The truth going to come out
Do not get exposed

Like

Congratulations you made it from a smart nerdy bomb
To a dumb nasty whore
It is funny
Where do you get off on telling people about themselves?

Everybody has their own styles and personalities
Get the hell off your high horse
Come back down to reality
Everybody deserves a chance to be loved

To be loved
To feel loved
Everybody deserves that chance

To have feelings for a person
To experience romance
Be careful who you judge
Be careful who you disrespect

Everybody deserves a chance
To be giving some respect
He/She could be ugly
Could be fat
Could be anything that you define as not being your type

Not beautiful

But

Can be the best spouse you ever had

Would not have

Or

Will have

 It is alright to have your type of people that you are into
That you like
It is alright to have standards
It is also okay to get out of your comfort zone and area

Love is love
Why people question that?

So

concerned about someone else's relationship

But

Where the hell yours at?

Being single is a choice
You should honor that
Some so confused about who they are into
What they want

It is okay
Love is moving around
Just not your way yet

To be loved
It come in all ways

Happy

Sad

Violent

Whatever you feel and makes you happy
That is love

Everybody deserves a chance to be loved

Everybody deserves a chance to be loved

I love you

You are loved

Behind The Glasses

There's a young man who's afraid to cry

Going through lots of feelings

He doesn't know why

There's a young lady who's afraid to express herself

Keep hearing no

Not knowing when she'll hear that yes

What lies behind the dark glasses?

Is it pain?

Are you ashamed?

Could it just be a style?

Do you think of yourself to be better than the next?

Do you have low self-esteem?

Behind the glasses there's a story

Hidden from the light and life

Smile to cover up your situations

Wearing dark glasses

Don't want nobody to see your eyes

Yet what is the truth?

Could it be a lie?

What lies behind the dark glasses?

Could it be happiness?

Could it be a style of fame?

Could it just be a style you wear all season long?

Behind the glasses are feelings

Emotions that people sometimes just don't explain

I know

I am one of them

Black

A boy with that melanin in your skin

You are beautiful

A girl with that smooth dark skin

You are beautiful

Black is beautiful in all shades

Embrace the natural

Feel good about yourself

If you cannot love and respect yourself

No one else can

Why mess up what took you so long to build up?

Your self-esteem

As beautiful as you are

You should not change a thing

Black men

We are cherished

Women love us for who we are

Let's stop trying to be something we are not

Look in the mirror

Tell yourself what you see

Keep a bold self-esteem

Say nobody is better than me

For

Black

Is

Beautiful

Beautiful and rich
Black is wanted
Black is needed
Black

Is

Beau-ti-ful

Black as Oil
Black as Cole
Black as the night sky in the country

Beautiful and pure
As the Gods and Goddesses
We were made to be

Light skin

Dark skin

We are all Kings and Queens

The creators and makers of all resources

Powerful than anything

A boy with that melanin in your skin

You are beautiful

A girl with that smooth dark skin

You are beautiful

Black is beautiful in all shades

Embrace the natural

Feel good about yourself

If you cannot love and respect yourself

No one else can

Blood

Don't get it confused

We could be related
That doesn't mean I claim you

DNA blood type
That makes us related
Same genes and everything

That doesn't mean a thing
Blood is blood
It runs cold sometimes
Yes we're blood

You're not family

Loyalty

Trust

Understanding

That's what makes a family
Not just saying we're blood

What's blood it you ask me

If you're so called blood family to some

You wouldn't tried

Or

Actually

Killed the ones you call your blood family

Blood don't run so warm in some family members veins

Going through life

You'll never be the same

Blood is blood

That's just a name to me

Call it what you want

Still doesn't mean anything to me

Loyalty

Trust

Understanding

Makes a family

Broken Mirrors

There is a young boy looking at me
 Right in the eyes
 He doesn't say nothing
Just stands there and cry

Each day he walks back and forward
Thinking about his life
Talking to girls passing him
Saying that could be my future wife

Everyday there's a fight
He passes the mirror everyday
Thinking about the next life
Head shaking

His soul is on the next flight
Trying to do right
Deep inside his broken mirror
Is the only reason he can't sleep at night

I told him to stop looking at himself
Better his self
You don't have to fight
Love yourself and say in the mirror this is my life

Clean Record

Decision is final

The sound of the gavel

17 years old boy has been free with a warning

The procession of a firearm

Drugs

Battery all thrown out

Just to be given another chance

To show what he's about

Straight A's

Honor roll

Star player in basketball

Hanging out with the wrong people

Almost got him some years in Juvenile

In court without a care

19 years old girls

First case after attempt murder and a police chase

10 years they all received

Two of them just made 18

Imagine having to spend your birthday behind bars

Research showed that only one of the girls been force and gone to trial

the next day

Let's just say she has a clean record

Just a price to pay

When will there be a time when people have their own minds?

Boys and girls catching cases at a young age

Most follow and afraid to lead

Be your own person

Even though you may stand in front of a judge

Even though you may on your own

Not telling you what to do or trick

The law has it's ways

You can have a clean record

A new start

Only if you show your heart

You can be heartless and have more records then hope

The system is only trying to get paid

You are letting them

The more you don't come clean and you're afraid

You're helping them

Drill

It's a drill

It's a drill

You out here in these fields

Mind so gone

You off these pills

Well let me spill

Until you feel that this gang life is real

You're a lame and punk

That clown told you what to do and you jumped

Just like the want to be gangs

Messed up

You bailey know what you're even claiming

It's a shame to lose your rep

Having another person tell you your steps

You lottery

Instead of you making money and living good

You so "Hood"

Never understood why the government would

Put more money into jails then into your pockets

Now I'm not putting gang members down

I'm not trying to make you feel low

It's just sad to see another body cold

Not having the chance to get old

Why you give your soul to the point you're 6 feet low?

We're already in hell

 A shame what few would do just for clout

But

Be careful what comes out of your mouth

Get caught up and you're going to your new house for it's a drill

It's a drill

It's not fair to the children who think it's cool

Not understanding that this is NOT what they want to do

It's a drill

But why?

Thinking about old times and how time flies

How we once looked up to see the sunshine

We shall make whole again

Until next time

Please stop the drill

Family Controversy

Crazy how family controversy happens

When we fight and disagree with our family

We can hurt each other in a fight

After some time

We will be alright

That is love

Sometimes we as families would not talk to one another for some time

Over something that happened or was said

We need to forgive them

Get over it

Sad how long people could stay mad

And

Be the main ones crying loud at the funeral

How mad can you be?

Like really stop it

Life too short to top it with more things they said or done

It is over

What was done is done

No need to act like you all love each other when the family comes

You should not let nobody take your joy

Family controversy will come and go

Man up

Woman up

And

Forgive

Your

Family

Flow

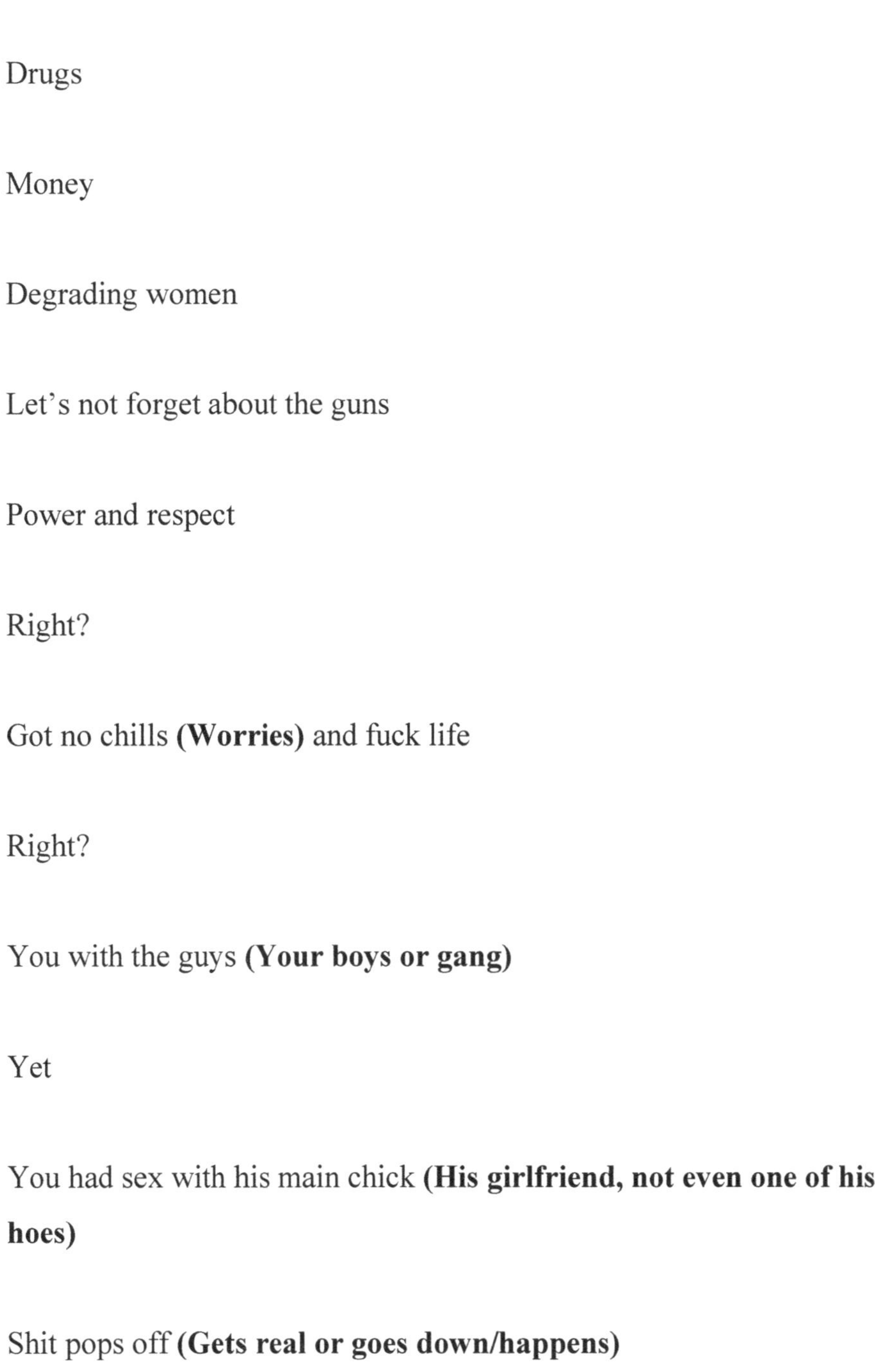

Drugs

Money

Degrading women

Let's not forget about the guns

Power and respect

Right?

Got no chills **(Worries)** and fuck life

Right?

You with the guys **(Your boys or gang)**

Yet

You had sex with his main chick **(His girlfriend, not even one of his hoes)**

Shit pops off **(Gets real or goes down/happens)**

Your guy the main snitch **(Talking to the police)**

You are tooting Poles **(Shooting or pointing guns)**

You in the kitchen

Right?

Whipping that shit up **(Crack Cocaine)** that's gonna hit the block

Right?

You are bagging it up **(Weed)**

That's your fast income **(Fuck a every two weeks paid check)**

Got caught by the dicks **(Polices)**

You say it's for no reason

You are checking bags **(Getting money)**

Not trying to flex **(Show out)**

You out here looking your very best

They don't know that's from your guys closet **(Wearing their clothes and shoes)**

You got a stain **(Robbed somebody)**

You hit that lick **(Robbed a business)**

Doing all these things just so you can feel rich **(Living in poverty)**

You ride you die **(Loyalty)**

Not even tryna survive

Shots goes off **(Shootings)**

Now watch them birds fly **(Somebody died or got killed)**

You so gang **(Gang member)**

Gang

Gang

In this bitch

Yet

Once your guys get locked up

Ain't no letters or money being pitched
(Just phone calls, but not putting money on their books or bailing them out of jail)

You hit the opps **(Opposite gang you are against)**

You caught a body **(Killed someone)**

Going around have sex with their girls **(Opposite gang girlfriends or hoes)**

My bad

I thought you was telling everybody

She let you crack **(Have sex with)**

Now you want to expose

Telling social media that she's a hoe

Bro that's disrespectful and just low

She didn't expose what she saw down below
(Not packing much dick or not knowing how to fuck)

None of my statements is the point

It's sad how we live life in a cycle

Just flowing around with no end

Talking about the same things that must end

I'll say let's get our lives together

Start flowing again

Positivity is the key with a new heart to love

If we need help

There's always a friend above

I Couldn't Be Even More Proud

If I don't have anything else to say to you

I want to say

I couldn't be even more proud

All the things you're going through

All the faith I didn't have in you

All the joy I took from you

Just having me crying

I couldn't be even more proud of you

All the times I didn't stand by you

All the lies I've told to you

Never would have thought you'll make it through

All the times I didn't look at you

Nearly bust mirrors cause of the sight of you

All I'll say is

I couldn't be even more proud of you

All the right that I made wrong

Not hearing you

Because of your tone

Just knowing one day you'll be alone

When I didn't give you hope so you could fly

I touch your hands and made you cry

I lost my faith and you laugh at me

You say a star I'll never reach

You stood by me and I stood small

I didn't have your love

I didn't have it all

So

I'm everything I am

Because

You hated me

Tried to defeat me

Beat me

If you were starving

You'll eat me

Now you're saying you couldn't be even more proud of me

Telling me to go for my dreams

Reach for the clouds

Man

You wild

I still remember when you threw in the towel on me
Thinking about when you said "You don't know how it is to be me"
Lowering my self-esteem from the ways you treated me
I mean you didn't want to have nothing to do with me

Now you're lost for words

All you can say is

You couldn't be even more proud of me

The whole time you're a part of me
I'm looking in the mirror crying so hard just thinking back
I made it so far
I smile in the mirror looking at a success story

Damn

I couldn't be even more proud

I Love Myself

I might be ugly
I just might be handsome

BUT

I love myself

I might be struggling
I just might be rich

BUT

I am surviving
I have something worth living for

I love myself
I do not need the criticism
I do not need the compliments
My name stay fresh in people mouths like a breath mint
Imagine Jesus fighting Lucifer
Red and White call that a peppermint

I love myself
I love myself deeply

Have not been in many relationships

Do not have many true friends

SO

Loving myself is easy

Everything about me I love

No exceptions

My flesh is a work of art natural in all ways

A masterpiece to be appreciated and notice

Not touch

Seem crazy

BUT

I learned to love myself

If I cannot appreciate all I have

Who I am as a person

How I look

Then I cannot expect other's to

My self-esteem is so high

I became bold about myself

SHIT

If I felt like Dennis Rodman did
I will marry myself
My personality is like unknown
I am floating on these haters
Call me the next best balloon

I love myself
Just like people love the next big thing
I am the next big thing
Great goals
Major dreams
I appreciate myself
I self-motivate myself
I love myself
I believe in myself
I love myself
I love myself deeply

I Wish

I'm getting older now
Thinking about what people told me

Never had time for fun as much
Now life is upon me

Wish I could go back
I'm the one people laughed at

Just wishing it had stopped
Didn't have many friends

Due to their crop
What a sight

Pictures painted
On my side is white

Not covered up
Never were

Wishing not to hear what I've heard
There were no doves

I'm the crow

I wish things could go back like they were

Before life hit me

Now the stories people heard

I'm good either way

I'm just wishing to end the cruelty

Thanks for what it done for me

It strengthened me

I'm A Winner

I'm a winner
Despite what everyone says
They'll be the same ones later kissing my ass

I focus on the future
Never forget about the past
It's thoughts like these that makes my heartbeat fast
Just like a thought it doesn't last

I'm an overcomer
overcoming the unknown
I know what it is
Who has time for their own tears though?

Yes
I'm
A believer

I'm sitting back and watching everything clearer

Yes
I
Could
Hear

Her

That voice in the wind wishing I'll just go my own way

For what I am?

Everything you ever thought I could and will be

I'm a

I'm a

I'm

A

Winner

I'm Different

It wasn't meant for me to follow

It wasn't meant for me to copy

I'm not trying to be like you

I'm not even sure if I like you along with wanting to be cool with you

You call me strange

You say I'm weird

I like the person I am

Is that hard for you to hear?

I'm different

Glad to be

Nobody can do me better than me

I'm different

Won't have it no other way

I'll love myself at the end of the day

I don't need to follow

I can lead

No need to copy

The only person I'm trying to impress is me

I don't need no friends

I don't need anyone

I'll stand out

That's how people know my name

I'm different

You don't have to understand me

You don't even have to love me

For you're not force into my decisions and lifestyle

I mean it's wild

Keep talking down about me

Disrespecting me

Why somebody just won't throw in the towel?

The fight is over

I tried to last the rounds

I've sored like a bird until I got shot down

I'm different

Love being different

For being different is how you get ahead in life

Is what people like

Just being yourself and loving yourself Is alright

I'm From

I'm from the weather is unpredictable

The people are unbelievable

If something goes wrong

It's just unreasonable

Trying to make a living

When violence is everywhere

People just don't care

Getting higher and drunker until there's no money to spare

I'm from the gays coming out

Leaders shutting their mouths

Some parents not reaching out

To know what their children are about

Trying to make a difference when there's no help and direction

People not trying to invest in dreams

It seems as we youth try to show progress

Just keep pressing and pressing

No one's impress

Until a "Nigga" confess and ends up behind that barbwire hell whole

I'm from the education system is no good

I mean people can learn basic skills in the hood

Now of days even a college degree can only lead you so far in life

So deep in those books that some don't even know about reality

Trying to earn a better education

No disrespect

What's the point?

You get so close then here comes the loans

Loans after loans

Pockets so empty that even the government want to be stoners

I'm from the truth

Speaking from the struggle

I mean having to work a double just so you can provide for yours

People trying to do right

Also trying to survive

Parents stressed every day

Some can't keep up with their kids

Few fathers not around

Happiness can't be found

I'm from the fake smiles

So many depressed

Trying to find joy when every day is a test

Hallelujah!

Thank you Jesus

The people cry

Crying for help to be saved before we die

I'm from the fights that turns into the shots

Educated teens just want to be on the block

Thinking you all are doing something
You all are not

I'm from young teenagers in gangs
Their English turned to slang
Posted with the guns
Drugs
Dirty money

Oh

What a shame

Trying to move forward in life with few people in your life
Seem as no one cares so you go to that street life
In our minds my generation is heartless and wants to be bold
Until "One of the guys" gets killed
Don't want nobody to see you all crying so you all fold

I'm from a place where it's ok for men to cry
To live your life however you want without being ask why
We're human beings

So

We live

We die

I'm from a place where lessons must be learned

Experiences is an everyday thing

The "Hood" or "Projects" isn't what it seems

I'm from a place where in darkness comes great things

In This Moment

Life was meant to be hard

It was meant to be enjoyed

You were meant to be happy

 It was also meant for you to feel sad

In this moment

You will feel all of that

In this moment

You will feel happy

Yet you will cry

You will get caught up

In this moment

Get sidetracked

Figuring out who you want to be

Thinking about your goals

Your dreams

Lost in the streets

Lost in the world

Lost in this moment

In this moment

So much is happening

Going on

What is right?

What is wrong?

In this moment

Every man for themselves

It is a war out here

Not world rumble

This is Black Ops

Killing and destroying Black Opps **(Opposites)**

Brothers killing brothers as the cops sit back and watch

In this moment

Everything and everyone are reckless

YES

Even the good ones

We all have something we are hiding

Until the dirt falls off us

Everything is coming to the light

In this moment

Who is to be trusted?

Your own love ones seeking for secrets to bust out

To help or to judge?

Turning your back on people

BECAUSE

Who and what they love?

In this moment
In your moments
Decisions to be made
Choices to take
Two roads

BUT

Which path to take?
Life isn't easy
Habits for the needs and wants

In this moment
Your life in a blunt held by Lucifer
Will you allow him to get high?

OR

Get your life together
That he chokes and dies

In this moment
Positivity is ahead

Inner Self

The way he walks

The way he talks

Makes an impact on people thoughts

The way he feels

 The way he heals

Make others wonder still

The knowledge that kills

Makes his whole life into a thrill

The way he enters your mind

You will think he is real

The way he jokes

Makes him everybody folks

The way he tells the truth

He is a hundred proof

Makes you wish you still had your youth

The way he fell

He is too smooth

Can you tell?

The way he looks

Got you hooked

Meet him one time

He will read you like a book

The way he lives

He might need a belt

It would not happen

Because

Of

My

Inner self

It's Just Around The Corner

A!

I have a question to ask

How do you want to die?

I know it seems so harsh and bold

Maybe mind blowing

Makes you think

Lives are giving and taking faster than you could get a thought in your

head

It is sad

So overwhelming when you think about it

If you decide to think

Thoughts maybe so far from your brain

Speechless

You cannot even blink

Death got you so still

Hypnotize

Cannot close your eyes

Visualizing life until you realize everybody going to die

It is not anything you will want to think about

Trying to clear your mind

I am not trying to scare you

I am not trying to make you afraid

I just feel that you should live your life to the fullest

No exceptions

Life and death are as real as it is going to get

Do yourself a favor

Live in your own way

I have a question

How do you want to die?

Tomorrow is not promise

Live now

Survive now

Enjoy life now

Death

It

Is

Just around the corner

Life

Emotions flow out my heart like water from a river
 Smacks against the rocks

It hurts

I'm hurt

Thinking about good times
The way you've played and smiled
Loved to enjoy yourself

Stayed true to yourself
If I had the chance to talk or write about another person
I'll still choose you
You were cool

Nobody could compare to you
Life can sometime be a bitch
Taking souls away fast
Who didn't deserve it
Death is coming

That's one thing for sure
Violence is not worth it

I never could understand

Why would you do the job of Jesus Christ

Who has the world in his hands

It hurts my heart and soul to mention names

So

I'll speak in general and say it'll never be the same

Life without you all will never be the same

Gone but never forgotten

Believe that

Gone but memories run in the mind like movie reruns

It's like it's over but never done

Life can sometime be a bitch

Taking souls away fast

Who didn't deserve it

Life is giving and taking in a blink of an eye

I'm staring at the pictures

Trying to be strong

All love and sympathy to the decease

Hard for me to say

But

Rest In Peace

Lights

I've once visualized dreams

To get a big break in life

To follow my dreams

Believe everything going to be alright

I've seen the lights in front of my eyes

Which one should I run to?

 I've gone through rejections

Put downs

Not even bringing up

When I got let down

On the road to success

No signs of stopping now

People say I'm going the wrong way

I'm heading to the light now

Spotlights

Which one I'm in?

Trying to get ahead in life

While committing all this sin

I once heard that my light will one day shine bright

Hopefully it'll be on my dreams

And

Not in this red light
Feel like I'm the target so point and say goodnight
Give me the green light

I'm ready to go right now
Go straight in
Play time is over with
No time to pretend

I've visualized dreams
Where in every lost I win
Feeling like T-Pain all I do is win

Win

Win

No matter what

But

Trying to turn a dream to reality is like being at gun point

So

I'll go my own way

With a little help

Shining my life out

It's like all lights on me when I step out

All eyes on me when I show out

People trying to keep me down

I'm not tapping out

I've once visualized dreams

Where I've accomplished everything

Can do anything

No need for introductions

I'm known as a young King

I've once visualized dreams

Where I've gone the wrong way

All about my grind

With dirty money in my face

Fine females around me

The whole world knows me

I've visualized

Me walking in the light

Without having to struggle

Without being let down

Only if I had more love and support

Will I felt everything would be alright?

It hit me and I realized

Once I open my eyes

Allowed the sun to come in

Dreams are over

Grinding to the top is where I've began

Motivation

Wake up every morning

AND

I grind to my best
Ain't no time for lacking when you trynna be the best

I'M THE BEST

Motivation got me on my grind
Got my own bills

JOB

MONEY

Please don't waste my time
Cause I'm going for mine
You could be motivated if you keep it in your mind
Being positive is all me
Mess with me I can change your whole life

AND

I PUT THAT ON ME

Motivation got me wanna speak to the nation

I wanna change some thangs

I wanna do some thangs

Cause I'm self-motivated

AND

I do my own thangs

I know y'all probably heard of me

IF NOT

THEN YOU WILL

I'm independent

AND

I keep it that way

Not saying I don't need nobody

BUT

People phony these days

SO

I GRIND

Not in these streets
Not on the block
I'm trynna provide for mine
Ain't no need for me to get shot
Wake up every morning

AND

I grind to my best
Ain't no time for lacking when you trynna be the best

I'M THE BEST

My Letter To My Father

Dear Father

I love you so

You are always here for me

No matter in a time of need or not

I am blessed

That is all I can really say

When it comes to my father

I am thankful

Grateful

You done what you were sat out to be

A father

You are my friend

With rules and regulations over me

I still remember them days

I will get in trouble

I was too old to not know how to tie my shoestrings

It is because of you I have learned to be peaceful

Calm

Maybe because I did not want a belt coming

Dear father

You are a lucky man
Taking care of six children with problems in your life
Things did not work out between you and my mother

YET

You stayed around
Came to see us every chance you have gotten
Never understood how you became so calm about everything
If you ask me
That is why I love you
Your energy and blood are within me

Dear father

I never could have found out how I am so good at rhyming
Until I have heard you rhyme
Spitting some off the wall kind of stuff
It was raw and made sense
Your talent stayed with me ever since
Father I know you feel that I do not listen to a word you say sometimes

BUT

I do

Hoping one day I will just be a piece of a reflection of you

Dear father

I am proud of you
Happy to be the son of you
Glad I had the chance and opportunity to stay a week at your home in
the country
I will be bold this time and say
Nobody could never compare to you

New Beginning

We can't be friends

We can't be cool

There's no conversation

I don't talk to fools

I don't address clowns

Not to be cruel or mean

You're a clown

You talk down about me

You've misused my name

Talking all this back in the days crap

We'll never be the same

You'll never be the same

Sorry you're late

Things has changed

I moved on

I'm moving ahead

I'll follow my heart

Forget what you said

I'm ahead

I trust few

I'm a struggling individual

Success I will find

I fell

Gone down

Still pushing for more

Even when people let me down

Glad most didn't stay around

No need to put hands out

When I was in need the help wasn't out

I started over

Made a new start

I have a new beginning

With a little heart

We can't be friends

We can't be cool

There's no conversation

I don't talk to fools

Survival

Didn't mean to dig up the past

But

My parents are the best role models I'll ever have

Six children
Three girls

And

Three boys
They raised together
In the projects

Problems after problems

But

We made it through

Six children
It didn't get any easier
Struggling after struggling

Our lives weren't breezy

It was a blaze
A blaze in hell

Shoot we prayed each day
Every night
Even having home church for our souls wasn't right

Barely got sleep at night
Listening to the unscheduled shootings we heard some nights

We made it a long way

But

By the grace of God

We survive each day
We survive every day
We survive the best ways we knew how

Life goes on

I didn't mean to dig up the past
Just remembering history

I'm the youngest

So

I could only tell you what I saw

What I heard

I'm the youngest

So

I didn't see everything
I'm guessing everybody was trying to hold it together for me

Well

I thank all of you

Title

What do you see?

Are you lost in what generations

After

Generations
Put in our heads

To divide us

To separate us

From the fact that we are more alike than you want to believe
If we were not never told to say we are colored and uncolored folks
What would we be?

Being a color is not a race nor a ethnicity
It is a color just like crayons
But for generations

And

Generations that is how we been separated

From our own identity and history

It is a mystery who were the first person on Earth
What was the complexion of the skin?

You can believe in whatever you want to
 Just do not put a title on me

I am just me

None Since

You're Black

You're White

Not losing no sleep

You shouldn't judge by race if you ask me

You're Gay

You're Straight

Bisexual and Confused

Stay true to yourself for you don't have nothing to lose

You're Tall

You're Short

Still lovable

Man

All these labels and names is unbelievable

You're Good

You're Weak

Good at different things

Just because somebody does it better don't mean a thang

You're Boney

You're overweight

Fat

Thick

Skinny

All sizes are great
So many people love you
Stop listening to people who hate

You're Dirty
You're Clean
All in between
People have personal problems
Help and stop putting people business out
Everybody has issues

Problems

Situations that we're dealing with

Believe it or not

Stop exposing and telling none since stuff
It's not everybody business to know

Help in all ways you can

Be that bigger woman or man and step up

If it's none since don't speak

We're all loved and so beautiful

Handsome

So

Take that power and do your thing

All love to the Kings and Queens

On My Block

If you haven't noticed
I'm a opp **(opposite)**

Talking to all gang members hoping the crime will stop
So many people look at me as flip flop

I never was in a gang
Just from two different blocks

Sad to say

I'm always hearing gun shots
The normal conversations are another one got popped

You cannot even visit your family members without being questioned
Just fuck with the right one
You're going to learn a lesson

Say the wrong shit if you are bad
You might just get popped
Hit so hard you are in shock
Your guys might have to help your ass

Because

It's not always nice on my block

People saying no lacking when it's hot
People lack all season long
They just not getting caught

That's not the point
That's the time when you would get shot
I mean body dropped
Somebody screaming

"Can you please stop"

I guess not

That child was with them when their opp's got popped
By a snake **(Trader)**

I mean how many does it take
To fight somebody y'all hate

What happens just happens
There's a reason

Hoping not to be hunted down all season long
Things should be mellow

Instead of being educated

We as a people dropped the books

Picked up the metal and steel

Can you feel the heartless ones that's ready to kill?

Please stop the drill

At least teach our youth the truth

So

One day they'll know how to make it through

Not the ways we were taught though

Teach them that so many people don't care about me and you

They just love and need us for what we can do

On my block you either is in or you not in a gang

If you are

I hope your life will change

To not live your life off clout **(Noticed)**

If something goes wrong someday

Your name is the only thing you can claim

Open Ears

I close my eyes

Open my ears

Knowing that so many are not here

I hear the stories

I heard the news

Trying to get over what others go through

Listen

Do not speak

Listen

They are taking our youth

You see it a little

That child got killed

Over what you do

It is a shame

The pain remained

Cause by the bath and stains

All over this gang stuff

It is truly messed up

Kids getting messed up
Over the mess ups

And men

Who decided not to step up

Please wake up
The times you shot
More of our race drop

Because

Instead of looking at that young man as a brother
You overlooked him as a opp **(opposite)**

Not even knowing if he was in a gang or not
You seen a chance and you shot

It must stop
I heard the fire
I heard the yell

I saw the tape
People faces

I saw the lights

Not being alright

To know that I

Alone with others may not make it through the night

People hear me speak

They suck their teeth

Saying

"You don't know how it is to be me"

I hear the tells

Along with you as well

The truth is

You will be better than your guys

If you do not rebel

Scream

All the things people say about me
I do not say much

All the things people do to me
I do not do much

Just keep my peace and remain calm
I remain calm

Hold my tongue
Lips never been so at rest

I try my best not to depart them
Don't test me

I am not hardcore
I am not even tough

Just do not fuck with me
I do not want to get you messed up

I will shut up
Not because I am afraid

It is just so much to live for
I want to see brighter days

Make a way for my people to be ok
Praying for this world to not go astray

Screaming

Why are the future dying?
We were the future

We could still be if the violent stop
If somebody catch the shooters

Shit crazy

We could have been famous without the News
Like Breaking News

You look up and the next big thing is gone from you
Gone from us

Screaming

Knowing teens cannot follow their dreams
Their spotlight in that red beam

Youth giving each other that one shot
The flash went off when their bodies dropped

Screaming

People talking all this good stuff
Actions we still have not seen

Got our asses feening for some weed
Thirsty for a drink

Rocking back and forward thinking about this economy
Shit just feeling like a dream

Caught in each other's steam
Madder than a Demon

We all are fighting against something

Sadly

How quick we rather blow something

People out here trying to catch a dream
Surrounded by these scenes

Acting like we all are with it

Shit

At least not me
Cause deep inside
All I want to do is scream

Shadow

There is something hunting me
It's my old lifestyle

I guess you could tell by the way I been acting

I don't know about you
I've been in the darkness
Trying to shine

My shadow

Oh

The memories

My shadow is behind me

So

I'll leave it there
Right along with my past

There were some things I was dealing with

For years

Just hoping it'll just go away

My shadow

You

Will

Not

Be

Missed

Just hoping it'll just go away

Stand Up

Names been called

Threats been made

Looking toward the sky

Hoping to see another day

Hands been drawn

Minds do not think the same way

People trying to make sure you are not seeing tomorrow

Trying to be a man

Yet comes to their level

Borrowing a gun

Making some calls

Brothers until somebody bowel to the law

Names been called

You are a number now

Could have still been around

If you just walked away

Words is just words

I know they hurt sometimes

It is not worth putting your life on the line

Over a statement

Just must be the tough one though

We need to stand up
Be the bigger person

Stand up
To just walk away
People are childish

Stand up
To take actions
This cannot keep happening
People do not like you for some reason
People lose their lives

And

End up behind bars over statements

Peoples opinion on you
It might be hurting you
Only if it is true
Get off their level
We need to raise up
If this is your daily life
Stand up

Starving

(If I was homeless, this what I will say)

Morning until late night trying to get this money
There is no difference from real and fake
People just walking pass

Sometimes fast

For the subway tunnels smell like I did more than just pass gas

Sometimes I wish this lifestyle did not last
Help needed and money comes in fast
If I get off my ass and entertain these people who just want a quick laugh

It is funny how people misjudged me
Just off my image and what they hear about me

Rich or poor we all are starving

Some just seem more
Talents are talents

I am more than a triple threat on the platform
You all are making it rain
I am making it storm

My clothes may not be the best
My shoes might look a mess
Do not look down on me
Sometimes that cold floor is home to me

That rough concrete
Them train carts
Just sleeping all around

Because

The shelters are hard
Sounds crazy but it is hard

You all claim to be in these streets
I live on them
Eat on them
Mostly starve on them
My kind die on them

Yes

I am fighting on them

Because

It is survival to the fittest

Starvation

The hunger games

The Struggle

Depression

Recession

And even

Recreation

Because

Poor people have fun too

I am not here for no handouts
Just want you all to hear the struggle coming out of my mouth
I speak through the pain
Not to be called a name

Because

If I was you
I would not do the same

So

Stop

With

The

Pass judgment

And

Pass enjoyment

The Norm

Laughing on a nice day

Where children once play under the treetops just to be in shade

The blaze from the sun burns you into a shade tone or two

Losing your breath from Johnny come across and other games

Years gone by and you are developing into a teen

8th grade was alright

High school is everything

It seems as you are stuck in the past

Fun times

No worries

Yeah

Your first kiss

Thinking about your childhood

All you could have missed

Getting wet

Hanging out

What new games and toys was coming out?

Now you are at a teen level
Really thinking into dating
Had girlfriends and boyfriends in grammar school
Those clowns you are hating

Fun

Fun

Fun

It is good you still have a child mentality
More of a sharper mind
You are a teen now

So

Whatever you heard is happening
You are exposed to a lifestyle that in your childish mind did not know
was possible

It is funny

You only been preparing without knowing

Of course

There are the friends who have been there

Love showing

Be careful

Middle school is where you made have lost your V card

Started gangs

There is nothing like thinking you know it all
Life will eat you alive like in a food chain
Do not be drawn that easy
Life is good for you now
You should continually shine

Decisions and choices are cold
Having to develop on your own
You do not know what is waiting for you behind that blizzard storm
This is not your childhood anymore
You are looking at the norm

The Road

There has been to many crossroads going on

In this lifetime

Some were people I know

The other ones were mine

Some made it

Other ones ran out of time

Trying to find that inner person at the peak of their prime

Man

It's too late now

You have time

The years you received

Your guys cannot find the money to bail you out

You could either serve or see the light

Thinking about that child who always had to fight

The lifestyle that led to being buck wild

Not crazy

Just

One of the guns for the hood

Because

If you put your guns down

What are you?

Messed up how we think

I was not always a great person

I was not as bad neither

I have been down so many roads

To tell you the truth

Going from a Church boy to wanting to be Gang

To a somewhat School boy and back to a Church boy

I understood what a man should be

Like when it came to the hood or block

But

The path that I take can change my life

Them Peaceful Waters

I've lost so many love ones
Just in a snap of a finger
Gone just that fast
Without saying my goodbyes
Hearing their last

Tears coming down my face
Thinking of the good and bad times
Smiling with joy
They no longer must struggle
Weep heavy for there will never be
Another one like them

Them Peaceful Waters
Flow so ever at peace
Tears end
Once the sunshine
Looking toward the sky
At that spirit line
Today will be a good day

Them Peaceful Waters
Slightly moves
Seeing my reflection in the water

My smile turned into a frown

As the splash of a tear drop hits the water

"Why they Had to leave so soon?"

Them Peaceful Waters

It's beautiful how the skyline meets with the body of water

If a had remains

It would've been a beautiful time to let the wind blow them away

Hard to say

But

They're gone

Looking over them body boxes

As

Their flesh reunites with the dirt

Trying to think about them peaceful waters

While

Hearing ashes to ashes

And

Dust to dust

Somebody please stop that Pastor
This all is too much

Them Peaceful Waters
Slowly I try to let go
Let them rest in peace
Trying to maintain my peace
Not cry out their names
So many good souls
Spirits departed this world
I wasn't ready to let go
I wasn't ready to see die
Just left so young without a tear to cry
They knew it was their time
I must be strong
Never forget of the ones

Who

Makes me sick
To know that
I must dismiss

I live

And

I will die

I look toward them peaceful waters
I try to survive

This Could Be My Last

Look crazy if you want

Make jokes if you want

Even call the nut house on me if you must

I am telling you that This Could Be My Last

This Could Be My Last day living

My last day seeing you all

My last day smiling or anything really

I could die tomorrow

Get locked up

Become famous

Even become rich

This Could Be My Last

I could kill myself

You know commit suicide

Focus on the important things in the world

To me it is pointless

I do not want to focus on things like that

When today

Or

Whenever I could die

I might be depressed

Stressed out

Crazy or anything else you could think about

I have every reason to be

Might be some of those things

It is a possibility

People is lost in the mind to me

Maybe I just think too deep

Either way

We have one life

Very few chances in life

Dreams to become someone in life

Do somethings in life

Short-term and long-term goals to reach in life

Only have few real people who are going to ride and die with us in life

Why waste it on something that is not beneficial to us?

Something our hearts not into

Life is simple

We always finding a way to make it hard

Life could be hard

Just look where we are at now

How much farther alone we came from

Life is simple if you ask me

But

Yes

Challenges and hardships will come
We can get through this together
One step at a time
We will never know what can happen to us in life
Good or bad

So

Let's make each day count towards something that we desire
We want to do and become in life
Beneficial to us and our families
If any or will be later in life

Why

This Could Be Our Last

Thug Rain

Young black boy making a living on his own

Struck out in life

All his chances are gone

Praying mother at home wishing he will leave the streets alone

No father figure in his life

He been gone

The streets heard it first before he did

Come to find out he's a one-night stand baby

His father didn't know

That's crazy pops

You could've tried to take responsibility

You know be the dad to your son

Then again you didn't know

So young and in so deep

Before he even turned a teenager

He was known in these streets

His gang was his family

So

They made sure he was fed

Stay getting paper

Clean

Slept in a bed

Anything and everything he wanted

Got his first child at 16
13 years old girl he knocked up wanted him to put his name on it

So

He continued to grind

Selling weed was his hustle
Had a strong relationship with his muscles

Hands

Fingers

Caught his first case with his daughter on the way
Having to see pictures in juvenile detention
Thinking he'll get love from his gang
They not showing him no attention

Thinking it's easy to just drop out a gang

Young boy was capping

Never really understood the saying "Ride or die"

Get out of juvenile one year early

Working with the cops

Receives news that same day about his name being hot

Back on his own

His baby mama gave him a chance

News traveled

Who can he depend on?

Kissed his daughter and baby mama for the last time

Years gone pass and he's been missing from the scene

Life finally hit him

Dead in the penitentiary

Young black boy making a living on his own

Struck out in life

All his chances are gone

Living a thug life sometimes it could rain

In too deep you'll never be the same

Struggles after struggles like a song in your brain

What a sad story about a thug in the rain

Time

24 hours nonstop

7 days in a week

525,600 minutes in a year

Think about it

How will you spend your time?

Who would you spend it with?

Seem like a long time

Think about time management

In life you have decisions and choices

To live as you were meant to be

Not what somebody wants you to do or become

525,600 minutes

How would you spend your time?

In love?

In pain?

In excitement?

In shame?

Whatever you do

Just remember time will remain

7 days weekly to live your life to the fullest

No matter how you decide to live it

What you do

Just spend your time for the purpose of you

No matter what you are going through

24 hours

365 days in a year

That is nonstop hours

Wasting your time to live a heartless life

I call that a coward

How dare you throw your life away

Living a violent lifestyle

That is not the way

Wasting your life before your prime

Think about it

24 hours nonstop

7 days in a week

525,600 minutes in a year

365 days in a year

How will you spend your time?

Who would you spend it with?

No matter what

Remember

The

Times

Times Change

It hurt me to hear the words slip from your lips

Just thinking about the times

How we slipped

Time change

I get that

Our bond I will miss that

Forever

Right?

That was the plan

Grateful we are still friends

It hurts

I am not going to lie

Just thinking about how time flies

Times Change

Yes

I get that

All this phony stuff
I was never with that
Throwing your life away
Yet you so smart

You said

"Bro just leave it alone"

I try to do my part
When a person seeking for help
It is hard

Times change

Yes

I see that

You surround yourself with people that got you acting strange

Well

You got the clout

You like the fame

Times Change

Well

It will never be the same
 Just hope I will be the same

Times change
I see how you got your name
Messed up
What you will do for a little cash

Times change
I am the one you cannot stand

Well

After all this time
We do not have to be friends

Unfriended

Ask me if I care

Ask me if I will think about it

Does it seem as if I am tripping over the situation?

I am not losing any sleep nor starving from starvation

I am just overwhelmed that it happened towards me

Now I can finally put you to the side with the other phonies

This is cause for a celebration

To know you are fiction

Living in fiction and nonfiction

Media made your mind friction

Electrifying

Living in data

Technology turned you into a true hater

So

Overwhelmed

Funny at that

You mad

I did not get angry

About you not being friends with me

Totally messed up in the head

Your life is an account

People logging in

People logging out

Trying to find out what you are about

That drama

Shaking my head

Laughing

Days gone pass and you are thinking about all I have done for you

Getting online seeing if you could friend me again

Very few chances with me

I already blocked you

Unwanted

Faces turn

Eyes moving up and down

Lifting noses up

The phony sounds

Making faces

Body language says it all

I was there before the success

Where are the hands when I am down?

UNWANTED

That is what I am

Now that you are all doing well

I never looked for a Thank You

Although I received a lot of Fuck You

Now that you are all so far in life

It is hard to look behind

RIGHT?

Success will take you places

Makes you forget about the ones who helped you

Actually

Cared about you

So be careful

Always remember the times

Like when we were broke and did not have a penny

Forget about a dime

The struggle hit us all differently

YET

I cannot remember even being told to keep my head up

UNWANTED

I can tell

Besides when you are all feeling low

Love is so much needed huh

Well not anymore

We're No Different

Special Ed

Down Syndrome

Even LD

What beautiful people to see and meet
I love them
I honor them
Even some my friends
Stories after stories from where I have begun

You slow

You dumb

Not going to know shit

It hurts more when you let it build inside you

Yes

It is true

I was in Special Ed and LD classes

Getting Picked on

Some teachers will say

"Awe you will get pass it"

So

I pass sick

Taking my anger out on everybody

For the education system is a bitch

People talked

People misjudged

When they gone through the same shit

Do not never look down on individuals

Due to their situations

We are no different

We all have problems

Issues

Situations

You batter not divide yourself from others

For respect is needed and will be given

This is not no time to lower somebody self-esteem

Keep doing that shit

Karma going to be your worst reality

We are no different

That is all I have to say

Treat others as you want to be treated

Tomorrow is one less price you'll have to pay

Welcome

The sun is shining

The wind is blowing

I am finally at peace

My soul is glowing

I see the plants

They are about to grow

Waiting for that colorful sight

Look at the birds

Sing and soar

All these creations

Are worth living for

I see families

Different races

Walking all directions

Smiles on their faces

Kids having fun

Even the pets can enjoy themselves

I love the sight of nature

If no one else

Beauty is beauty

That is what makes it beautiful

The sight of your eyes

Is your opinion

What you decide to define

As beautiful

Feel the unity

Hear the harmony

Touch the natural

Smell the scent

Taste the crops

See the visual

Earth nature is not always what the human eyes visualize

In every good thing

Bed thing

Something beautiful comes out of it

So welcome

To what I visualized

Hope you can invite me

Inside of your eyes

White Child

Dear white child

I love you
You are my friend
I care about you

A white child
I love your style
Things be too fitted
Your personality is wild

It is wild
How we try to trade places
Living as each other
We are in two different places

You all want what we have
We want what you all have
It is simple no need for math
Some Blacks want to be White

AND

Some Whites want to be Black

I do not believe in that shit

We are all humans

We love different things

White child

There is no need to be or try to be something you are not

We all have our time to shine once the light hit our spot

Who Are You?

Do not be ashamed
You were made to be you
The person you imagined
Should be gone from you

The money it took just to find you
You should be looking in the mirror
See the real you

It is up to you
All I am saying is that you are beautiful
That you are handsome

Take pride in yourself
Be that person you were made to be

So I ask you
Who are you?

Do not let items make you
Do not let looks change you

TALKING THAT SPIRITUAL

Bending Knees

My father who are in heaven

I come to you in shame

I have done some things that left you in pain

Sinning on a daily basic

While still saying your name

Hopefully not in vain

You have looked down upon me and it rained

The flood gates are not open

Blessings I barely received

Trying to better myself

When

Life said I cannot achieve

I am on bending knees

Not taking a knee

Devil you are not my coach

I am on the wrong team

People said it is ok to be lit

To be on fire

I am on both knees

Nearly

Speaking in tongues to lift your name higher
I am a man
I am not perfect
You died so I can have the rights
To the tree of life
I am a man
I will fall short of your grace
Your mercy
Sometimes

I am on bending knees
You once said

"If I be lifted, I'll draw all men unto me"

I am praying to be at the right-hand side of you
You all I need
Every breath you breve through me

And

Each time it is a do over
Thinking about them nights when I lay my head
Just hoping it is not my death bed

I am on bending knees

I want to leave paradise knowing I have lived my life to the fullest

Serving your purpose Lord

I repent Lord

I have gone down the wrong path

Lucifer and I almost became friends

I am on bending knees

Thinking about what God has for me

Seeking his glory

Was in tears when I shared my story

I put it all on the alter

And

Left it there

I gain my V I C T O R Y

I am on bending knees

Thank you for all you have done

About to do

Even when I am going through

I know you will see me through

It is already done

I am on bending knees
You gave your only begotten son
Images pops in my head
Trying not to see the blood run down
You love us so much that you died
We all are sinners

I am on bending knees
Jesus is alive
I am just grateful
He is helping me to survive

GO In God's Peace

I finally see things clearly

Walking by faith as life fear me

God can you hear me?

Are you the reflection of whom speaking?

Have I been talking to myself all this time?

Think I should rewind to the history that is hard to find

We were once Gods and Goddesses

Ruling the land

Every resource was in our hands

Kings and Queens what happened to us?

History is only a cycle

No need to turn back the hands of time

History repeats like a beat and blood drop wine at my feast

It is time for the harvest

I am history

My body is a mystery

Just gone out the picture with no trace

God's face is a reflection in the mirror of whom we hate

Souls we take

Leaving a trail in time with no pace

Just running on through life

I need some space

It feels like everything is caving in

I cannot see my face

Just that solid mirror that will not break

I have seen the last glimpse of my reflection before the dust passed over

Not deserving to see the image of myself betrayed me

Knowing that I am just a reflection of who made me

Whom is my maker?

Inside of me is a creator

I have created my peace

Sitting at the table preparing for the feast

I am a King

Not King Jesus

I am God made into his image

And

I shall go in peace

Healed

My health

My soul

My state of mind

The point that I'm healed

No worries to find

I'm poor

I'm middle-class

I'm rich

I'm healed

From the top of my head

To under my feet

May not have everything I want

Yet

I'm healed

Healed in my soul

Healed in all ways

I'm

Healed

I'm Blessed

I don't have everything I want

BUT

I'm blessed

I may not be where I would like to be in life
In my career

BUT

I'm blessed

I'm blessed

BECAUSE

I say I am
I believe it

I'm blessed

I focus on the positivity
Put it in my mind I never heard of negativity

I'm blessed

I'm receiving the blessing
Share them among the believers and nonbelievers
Every day is a day of Thanksgiving for me
God's been so good to me
Every day he's blessing me

Death is daily
Marriage is a maybe
Birth is a beautiful thing
After enduring the pain

"Shower down a blessing"
Quoted by my brother in Christ Kirk Franklin
Melodies From Heaven sound good in my ears

I'm blessed

I have a reason to be
Thinking about life
What few people done for me

I'm blessed in the going in
I'm blessed in the going out
I'm blessed on the outside

I'm blessed on the inside

Blessings are all in my life

I'm blessed

Wondrously blessed

I won't complain

I'm blessed

"I'm blessed in the city

I'm blessed in the field

I'll be blessed when I come

AND

When I go"

In the encouraging words of my brother in Christ Fred Hammond

I'm blessed

Don't mean to start quoting songs

BUT

When I look back over my life

AND

I think things over

I can truly say that I've been blessed

To my brother in Christ Donald Lawrence

Thanks for the message

FOR

"I will be blessed indeed and enlarge"

My territory is flooding with blessings

Say what you want

Try to Stone me

I'm feeling like New Direction

"I got the Victory"

AND

Soulful for victory today is mine

I look at negativity

Tell Satan to get behind me

I'm blessed

BECAUSE

I'm alive

I'm blessed

BECAUSE

I've survived

I'm over joyful
Jesus is the reason why
I might feel down sometimes
I might break down and cry

BUT

Just like my brother in Christ Norman Hutchins once said

"God got a blessing with my name on it"

I'm blessed through it all
People want to know how and why questions

BUT

My answer will always be I'm blessed

In The Mix Of It All

I once was the shameful

I was not afraid to lie

I try to live my life to the fullest

No telling when I will die

I keep my head high

Spread my arms

I feel like I could fly

I am standing on my thrown

With my head held high

Looking toward the nation

We are all just some survivors

Surviving to live

Live for more

We are to be disappointed

We are going to be let down

We are going to fall sometimes in life

BUT

We make it in the mix of it all

The Devil is waiting

Your soul he's taking

As soon as you give up

Let go in life

Not saying you must believe

It is greater things waiting for you

We are not losers

Life is not a game

The levels just get harder sometimes

In the mix of it all

We must be stronger

Be the soldiers in war

We are going to be disappointed

We are going to be let down

We are going to fall sometimes in life

BUT

We make it

We survive

In the mix of it all

One Word Away

I hold my breath

Think about my actions

Don't want my name to come up

If something happens

Front page

All the News channels

I just need some strength Lord

These things I can't handle

So

I'm flipping the channels

Of

Myself episodes

Seeking your words for I'm out of control

Barely surviving

No telling when I'm dying

I reached out my arm

Extended my hand

For I'm weak

You make me stand

Strong and mighty
Yet so poor
No turning back
I'm fighting for the Lord
On this battlefield
Called the world
Where I'm fighting life

My Lord

My Savior

Jesus Christ

The reason I think about life
For he gives
He takes
I'm just so happy
To see another day

For there're those who gone before me
Completed the race
Fought their last fight
Dying with a smile on their faces
Their suffering is now over

My Lord

My Savior

My reason of being

My everything

 I am one word away from clearing my sins

But

There's so many
Where do I began?

I'm one word away from going back to my old ways

But

You yelled from the heavens
Said I'll be ok

You once said this battle is not mine
It's yours to fight

Yes

I once was poor
Now I'm living find

Yet

You never came when I needed you

But

You always on time

I am one word away
From thinking about the past

Live for today

Your grace

Your mercy

Your honor

Your faith in me
Let's me know there's brighter days
Like when I don't have the resources to make it through day to day
You told me to have faith
For I know in my heart you will make a way

I'm one word away

From two different paths

One choice

Never been so humble

Until I heard your voice

I was going for the fame

Trying to get a name out there

All it was doing

Was leaning toward them flames

I must wait

For my time is coming

Looking toward the heavens

I'm in the spotlight

When

I walk in the light

That beautiful light

Shine all around me

By day and by night

Because

Jesus the light of the world

He's ever shining

I'm in between reaching my goals

And

Money that folds
Doing it the right way
Yeah it blows

But

This is the life I chose
Being blessed
Successful
I know Jesus loves me

And

Blessings overflows
Keep the faith
That's what I've been told
I am who I am
He lives in my soul

So many choices
Just to be real or fake
I'm thinking too much

Don't feel like I have all day

But

All I am

Is

One

Word

Away

Pure

Lord I stand here today

I'm a sinner

From the moment that the doctors told my mother to push

And

There I've enter

A world full of sins

I just want to be pure Lord

I can't pretend

My parents created me

I was birth into this Devilish world

I just want to be pure

No matter how much of a church boy I am

I'm still doing wrong

Like who am I?

I'm not pure

I'm seeking to be

I'm not done with my race

Trying to be careful Lord

I wake every morning
Falling short of your mercy

Your grace

Every day is a new day
A day I could start over
Thanking you Jesus for how I got over
Praying one day I'll be made over

I just want to be pure
To live my life according to your will

Your plans

I don't want to live if you're not by my side Lord

In my life Lord

In my soul Lord

When I die

Where I'll go Lord?

My parents told me about you
You continue to lead the way for me

If I never trusted in you Lord

I wonder what kind of man I would've been today

Lord I just want to be pure
For you to continually to live and move within me

Reborn

I looked in the mirror
You I have seen
Thinking about our time together
How you were a part of me

We together damage some things
I gone down in that water
You did not follow me

Being reborn
I looked back
Noticed the demon inside of me
Damn did it feel good

But

The choice came
Both was fighting when the lighting came
They spoked my name
Both pulled and I felt the pain
The fire hit the clouds and then it rain
Everything cleared up
I was the remains

Step Aside

I've done my best

That's all I can do

Now I'll step aside so you can see me through

In the darkness is where my soul dwell

Seeking for a light in all this hell

I felled to yell

Screaming in my mind Emmanuel

For the Lord is with us

Even during our sins

No need to feel ashamed

We shall yell to the heaven Jesus name

For I'll step aside

Let you do your works

For the last thing you'll want to see is your children hurt

I'll step aside and let you fight

For deep in my heart everything is alright

I'll step aside

For you are all mighty

Power in your hands

You touch me with a finger and my soul feels happy again

I'll step aside for you are the great I am

Your greatness inside let me see anything as a victory

You saw the best in me

When I've seen the sins

My life was like a story coming to an end

I felt hurt so my knees will bend

Blessings after blessings I'll step aside again

Within Jesus I found a friend

Surrender

I stand here before you

With my arms stretched wide

Head toward the sky

With my mouth open wide

Screaming

JESUS!

The silent began

The atmosphere is still

Lights became dim

As spirits move over me

It is time

FOR

Confessions

I put my hands together

They started to shake

My fingers moved closer together

I felt the pressure

OF

Gravity pushing me to my knees
My lips formed to say three words

"I need thee"

I spilled out my problems
You already knew my sins
I guess you was just waiting for me
To come back to you again
Seemed so simple

YET

It was so hard to pray

TO

Heal my heart

TO

Learned from my ways
I made mistakes
Had bad habits that was not easy to break

Sources

All related to Spirituality

SO

I kept the faith
Prayed sometimes
In all I have done
One thing for sure
My life has changed

SO

I surrender to you

NOTES

About The Author

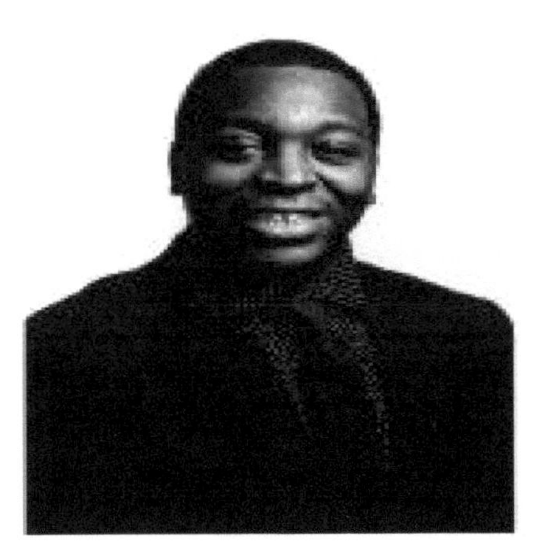

Lavell Harris, better known by his stage name Eli Sankofa, is an American Poet, Author, Entertainer, Inspirational Speaker, and Entrepreneur. Being raised in humble beginnings, Lavell is the youngest of three sisters and two brothers.

With the help of both parents and five older siblings, Lavell inherited numerous talents. These skills include Singing, Rapping, Acting, Dancing, Comedy, and Writing with so many more. However, in 2011 Lavell found writing as a way of coping with life. Lavell later found his way as a published author in 2016 one year after graduating from Dunbar Vocational Career Academy, and continues to make history through his work.

NOW AVAILABLE:

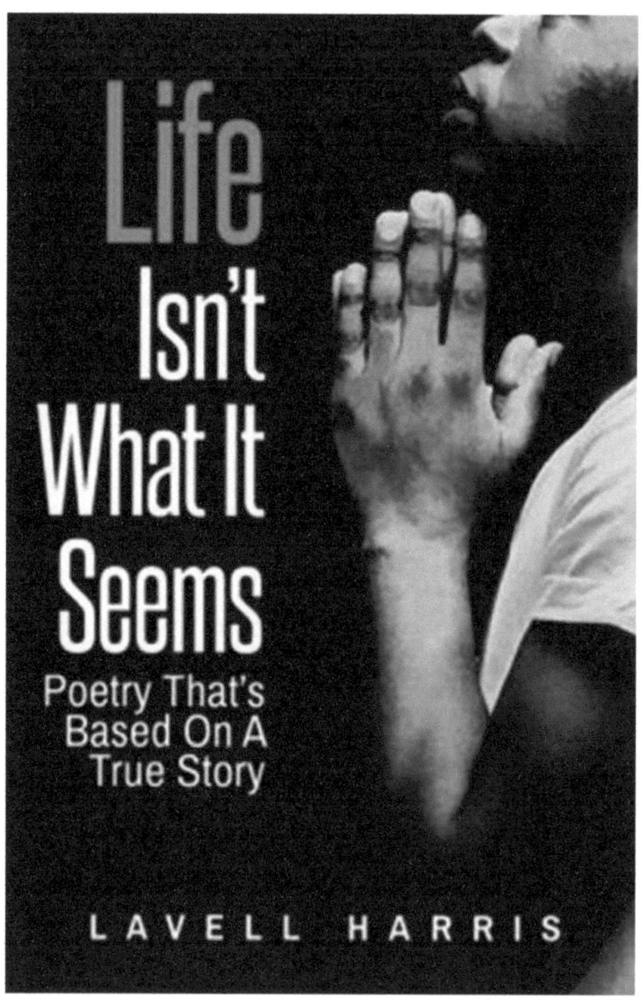

Printed by Libri Plureos GmbH in Hamburg, Germany